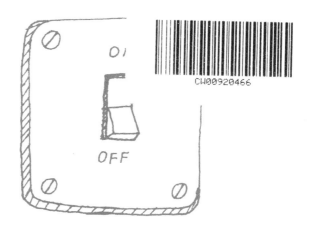

Flipping a Switch:

Your Guide to Happiness and Financial Security in Later Life

Barbara O'Neill, Ph.D., CFP®

2020

FLIPPING A SWITCH: YOUR GUIDE TO HAPPINESS AND FINANCIAL SECURITY IN LATER LIFE

Printed in the United States

PROJECT MANAGER: Katie Cline
INTERIOR LAYOUT AND JACKET DESIGN: Nicole Sturk

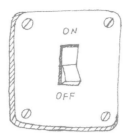

Dedication

Flipping a Switch is dedicated to Dr. Anthony Fauci, director of the National Institute of Allergy and Infectious Diseases at the National Institutes of Health, to whom the United States owes a huge debt of gratitude for his work in fighting the COVID-19 pandemic. Dr. Fauci did not flip the work-to-leisure "switch" years ago, when he easily could have. Rather, he has continued to use his expertise to inform the public and save lives. Dr. Fauci is a role model for all older adults who want to continue to make a difference using their knowledge, skills, passions, and time.

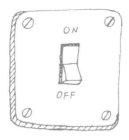

Table of Contents

PART 1: Financial Transitions

PART 2: Social Transitions

PART 3: Lifestyle Transitions

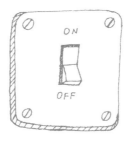

Foreword

I so often hear from people who are worried about how they'll plan and invest for retirement, how they'll pay off debt, how to save for emergencies, how to save for their kid's college education, and more. As CEO of the Investor Protection Trust (IPT) and Investor Protection Institute (IPI), I work tirelessly with my team in creating noncommercial, educational programs and resources to help people grow and protect their wealth. Throughout my career, I have had the privilege of meeting others who do the same. No one exemplifies an educator and champion for financial and investor education more than Dr. Barbara O'Neill.

As people navigate the retirement landscape, which seems to be ever-evolving, this book is so timely, starting with the title. For me, *Flipping a Switch: Your Guide to Happiness and Financial Security in Later Life*, encapsulates what retirement should be: acknowledging that your life is changing, you deserve happiness after a long career, and you still have financial obligations, some of which you have never experienced previously. In addition to exploring well-known but often misunderstood topics such as how to withdraw retirement savings, Medicare, and taxes, Barbara also brings to light other topics many may not be thinking about (or struggle with) as they approach retirement such as investing later in life and how to best live your retirement years.

Barbara has impressed me over the years with her ability to take a wide range of financial and investor education topics and put them into concise highlights (or bullet points) to educate not only her students but her colleagues, peers and the rest of her vast network. One way she does this is through her tech savvy, using social media and other digital platforms to share presentations, conference takeaways and other lessons learned. I admire her passion to keep learning, something all of us should do, especially in our later years. After an illustrious career as Distinguished Professor and Extension Specialist at Rutgers University, she is pursuing an encore career, which includes writing this beautiful book. She is seeking purpose and meaning by continuing to teach through the written word and provides thought leadership and advises many organizations similar to IPT and IPI, including the Association for Financial Counseling and Planning Education (AFCPE), where she created the Mary O'Neill Financial Education Mini-Grant in honor of her mother. Through this book, she expands well beyond what the Twitter character limit allows to create a comprehensive guide for people of all backgrounds and phases of their financial journey. This book is not just for those in retirement or approaching retirement. It is for anyone planning for retirement. In other words, it is for all of us.

Barbara has also been a champion of *When I'm 65*™ (www.wi65.org), a public television documentary and national engagement program which utilizes a multi-generational approach to examine how each generational cohort is looking at and planning for retirement, using case studies, engaging animations, and lively expert interviews. The program offers a toolkit with videos, booklets and action guides, supporting many topics covered by Barbara in this book. Some of the topics include rules for required minimum distributions (or the Mandatory Flipped Switch, as Barbara puts it), Social Security, healthcare, a new definition of retirement, and how to protect your nest egg. Investor education programs like *When I'm 65* work best when the content and toolkit resources are put in the hands of educators like Barbara who find creative ways to share the content, incorporate it into lessons and workshops, and deliver to communities locally on a grassroots level, statewide and nationally.

I appreciate that Barbara puts emphasis on investor protection in this book by highlighting fraud and the importance of protecting your assets. She does this especially in the chapters *Becoming Fraud Bait* and *Handling Wildcard Events*, which include a discussion of diminished capacity. Since 2010, we at IPT have run the Elder Investment Fraud and Financial Exploitation (EIFFE) Prevention Program, a training program for medical professionals and lawyers to help them educate and protect their elder patients and clients. We help them recognize when their older clients may be vulnerable to or victims of financial abuse, particularly those with mild cognitive impairment, and then to refer these at-risk patients to State Securities Regulators, local adult protective services professionals, or other resources.

Just as it is important to start saving and investing as early as possible, it is also important to start early in learning how you can become vulnerable as you age. In that process, you learn how to put things in place to protect your money, such as estate planning, wills, power of attorney, ways in which to control your hard-earned dollars, and so forth. You learn about the many types of scams, which increase and change every day. You also start talking to family and close friends early and often so you can look out for each other.

As you turn the next page of this book, think about how you will turn the next page on your path to financial freedom. What chapters are in your future? What should you be doing (or not doing) now so your future self can enjoy your later life? I know these questions are heavy and overwhelming. But Barbara wrote this book to guide you. I encourage you to listen to her.

Don M. Blandin
President and CEO
Investor Protection Trust (Investorprotection.org)
and Investor Protection Institute (iInvest.org)

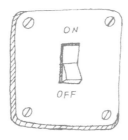

Introduction

You might be wondering what happiness, financial security, and light switches have in common. Quite a bit, actually, as you will see in the chapters ahead. Happiness and financial security in later life often require a 180 degree turn from the way people previously managed their time and money. A good analogy is "flipping a switch" because many changes are sudden and "on/off" (e.g., working one day and not working the next). Another good analogy is a "dimmer switch" for transitions that happen in stages (e.g., phasing out of paid employment gradually).

At perhaps no other time in life do more "switches get flipped" than when people leave a long-time career after working for decades. This is especially true for baby boomers who may have never experienced adult life without a full-time job. Many need to stop or reverse activities they have been doing since their 20s. Some switches are voluntary, like spending accumulated savings, and some are mandatory, like taking required minimum distributions (RMDs) starting at age 72. Some financial decisions are complex and may require research or assistance from professional advisors.

Three separate but related events informed my "flipping a switch" analogy. First, I was preparing to leave my career as a Rutgers University professor and personal finance specialist after 41 years of service. Upcoming life transitions were suddenly coming off the back-burner and into clearer focus. Next, there was a presentation about spending in retirement at a 2018 American Savings Education Council (ASEC) meeting. The speaker, ASEC CEO Lori Lucas, described a subset of retirees with a unique "problem": they saved their whole life, are not comfortable spending down their savings, and keep growing their assets. She noted that "we need to teach people how to 'flip a switch' from saving to spending in later life."

Lastly, on my way to the aforementioned ASEC meeting, I read an article called "Grasshoppers and Ants in Retirement" in the *AAII Journal*. The article referenced the Aesop's fable about the carefree grasshoppers that party on obliviously while conscientious ants gather food for winter. A key takeaway was that lifetime spending habits, whether they lean toward spending or thriftiness, are difficult to break. The academic term for this is the "habit formation hypothesis." "Ants" spend less in later life than they are financially able to. I realized that I was an "ant" and would personally find it challenging to "flip a spending switch" and see account balances decrease after 50 years of saving (since my teens).

Next came the realization that there are many "switches," beyond the financial, to flip after decades in the labor force. Whether people adhere to FIRE (Financial Independence, Retire Early) principles and plan to quit their jobs during early middle-age or they leave a full-time career sometime in their late 50s or 60s as most people do, there are dozens of financial and life transitions that occur. I started doing research and interviewed friends and colleagues who shared valuable insights. Eventually, I identified 35 financial, structural, social, and emotional transitions.

What stood out, clearly, is that most older adults do not want a life of "pure leisure." Rather, they crave a sense of purpose, meaningful daily activities and relationships, and the freedom to do what they want, even if that means continuing to work. Thanks to health and medical advances, some people will live 25, 30, even 40 years after leaving their final employer. FIRE proponents could live even longer. These so-called "bonus years" are a relatively new phenomenon compared to the shorter life expectancies of generations ago. They afford an opportunity to try new things, "reinvent yourself" with meaningful activities, and build wealth through additional decades of compound interest.

I wrote this book to help others like myself navigate common transitions and decisions as they flip their switches. Over 70 million baby boomers have transitioned, or will soon be transitioning, from full-time work to new pursuits, and millions of younger Americans aspire to do so. Many are unprepared for what comes next, both financially and emotionally. For example, defined-contribution plans such as 401(k)s have largely replaced defined-benefit pensions, making it necessary for previously employed workers to create a simulated "paycheck" from savings withdrawals, Social Security, and other income sources. On the life planning side, there have been numerous reports about boredom, depression, and isolation accompanying a lack of sense of purpose after full-time employment ends. This is a very serious issue because loneliness might even be a bigger health risk to older adults than smoking or obesity!

This book is organized into three parts: financial transitions, social transitions, and lifestyle transitions. Each aspect of an older adult's life involves numerous "flipped switches," not all of which are pleasant (e.g., becoming an "elder orphan") or within our control (e.g., RMD income tax rules). However, many switches are positive, such as taking trips that you dreamed about for years and making philanthropic lifetime gifts and watching the recipients benefit from them. All three life domains are also related. Finances, for example, influence relationships (e.g., ability to travel to visit family members), lifestyle decisions (e.g., moving to a smaller home), and health (e.g., healthy habits and access to health care).

In Part 1, *Financial Transitions*, you'll learn about developing a "permission to spend" mindset, accepting the fact that you "have enough", creating your own "paycheck," taking required minimum distributions, collecting Social Security and Medicare, simplifying your finances, and more. In Part 2, *Social Transitions*, you'll learn about options for meaningful daily activities, how to answer the "What do you do?" question, and how to navigate relationships with and commitments to family members and friends. Part 3, *Lifestyle Decisions,* will discuss a wide variety of "flipped switches," including downsizing possessions, "return on life expectancy" calculations, new definitions of success, factors associated with happiness in later life, and "wildcard" events, such as sudden wealth via inheritances, loss of a spouse, and physical or cognitive declines.

Everyone has their own unique "switches" to flip, so think of this book like a menu in a diner in my former home state of New Jersey. Walk into any Jersey diner, and the menus are thick, and the dessert cases are full. You cannot possibly eat everything, so you pick and choose. Similarly, this book offers a variety of ideas for you to ponder and/or act upon. My hope is that your "switches" will flip a bit more easily as result of this book and that you will be healthy, wealthy, and happy in the years ahead.

References

Finke, M., Guo, T. & Johnson, R.R. (2018, June). Grasshoppers and Ants in Retirement. *AAII Journal,* 23-24, 29 https://www.aaii.com/journal/article/grasshoppers-and-ants-in-retirement.

Kurt, D. (2019). Retirement and Depression. *Investopedia* https://www.investopedia.com/articles/retirement/120516/retirement-and-depression-6-ways-overcome-it.asp

Loneliness Might be a Bigger Health Risk Than Smoking or Obesity (2017). *Forbes* https://www.forbes.com/sites/quora/2017/01/18/loneliness-might-be-a-bigger-health-risk-than-smoking-or-obesity/#2e217aeb25d1

White, R. (2019). Is Your Defined-Benefit Pension Safe? *Investopedia.* https://www.investopedia.com/articles/retirement/08/safe-db-plan.asp

PART 1: Financial Transitions

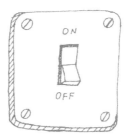

Chapter 1: If You Don't Spend Your Money, Someone Else Will!

Full disclosure—this chapter and several others are written from a vantage point of privilege. A majority of American older adults will not be "flipping a switch" to spend down six- and seven-figure sums after decades of saving. The reality is that many have little or no savings set aside for later life expenses and will struggle to make ends meet in their "golden years." According to the 2019 Retirement Confidence Survey (RCS) by the Employee Benefit Research Institute (EBRI), only 66 percent of U.S. workers or their spouse have saved any money for their final decades of life. This means that 34 percent of workers—1 in 3—have saved nothing, nada, zilch. The RCS also found that only 61 percent of workers are currently saving money to supplement Social Security and/or a pension after they leave the workforce.

Even more troubling are the amounts being saved for life expectancies that could run into the late 80s, 90s, or beyond. According to the EBRI RCS, 40 percent of workers reported that the total value of their savings and investments, excluding a home and defined benefit pension, is under $25,000, including 19 percent who have saved less than $1,000. Using the popular "4 Percent Rule" for asset withdrawals that last 30 years, $25,000 of savings would translate to just $1,000 of annual income ($25,000 x .04) or $83.33 per month. This is hardly enough to pay a weekly grocery bill, let alone other living costs. Almost 1 in 5 workers (19 percent) have saved $100,000 to $249,999, and 23 percent have $250,000 or more. It is this latter cohort, particularly those who have saved $1 million or more, that *Flipping a Switch* was written for.

So why is it so hard for people who have been prodigious savers to start spending down? As noted in the introduction to this book, old habits developed over a long period of time can be very difficult to break. According to the habit formation (a.k.a., habit persistence) hypothesis, people become accustomed to living a certain lifestyle that is tough to change when their income and/or assets change. "Ants," who have followed advice to be frugal and "save, save, save" for decades, can be hesitant, therefore, to suddenly turn on a spending spigot, even though they have sufficient savings to do so. One study found that those with substantial assets are the most reluctant spenders. Another found that those in the top wealth quintile spent nowhere near an amount that would place them in danger of running out of money. Even when forced to withdraw money from tax-deferred savings accounts for required minimum distributions (RMDs), starting at age 72, many habitual savers simply turn around and reinvest the money into new taxable accounts.

The transition from "accumulation mode" to "distribution mode" (i.e., spending and gifting) can be a landmine for people who have trouble "letting go." A big mental obstacle for "ants," in addition to their frugality and ingrained savings habits, is conditioning over many years to see their savings and investment account balances go up. Sure, they experienced losses (at least on paper) during the early 2000s "Tech Bubble" and the 2007-2009 Great Recession, but they most likely waited these market downturns out. They will likely do the same thing during 2020 market volatility related to COVID-19. What's more, savvy investors kept purchasing additional shares when stock and mutual fund prices decreased by following a dollar-cost averaging strategy (i.e., purchasing regular dollar amounts of securities at regular time intervals, such as $100 of stock per month or 8 percent of pay in a 401(k) every pay period). In other words, they invested when securities were "on sale." When financial markets eventually rebounded, these patient "ant" investors were rewarded for their foresight and patience.

Spending down savings in later life is different than experiencing periodic bear markets. Instead of "riding out losses," money is actually withdrawn and, as a result, account balances decrease, perhaps permanently. To conscientious "ants," seeing less money than they had before can feel like a market loss. A study published in the *Journal of Personal Finance* in 2018 explored the psychology behind later life spending decisions and found that half of the survey respondents agreed with this statement: "The thought of my retirement portfolio balance going down over time brings me discomfort, even if the decline in value is a result of me spending money on my retirement goals." Uncertainty about stock market performance and future health care and long-term care costs were also associated with retirees' reluctance to spend down their savings.

- **Admit That You Are an "Ant"**—Recognize the signs and current effects of your ingrained spending and saving habits. For example, take note of buying items at deep discounts, bragging about frugal habits, flying coach when you can afford business or first class, saving tax refunds, and gifting and/or tipping modestly. Keep a cash-flow journal and record decisions that you make and emotions that you feel when you spend or save money.

- **Step Outside Your Comfort Zone**—Practice spending on "big ticket" items. In 2018, I bought two tickets to the Broadway musical *Hamilton* when I had time to attend a play during the holidays. As the online Ticketmaster purchase clock counted down from 10 minutes, I agonized over this purchase until I finally clicked "submit." On the day of the performance, we spent another almost $200 for a prix fixe lunch at Rockefeller Center. What I remember now is a magical and enjoyable experience that far exceeded any "pain" caused by spending more than $1,000 that day.

- **Answer Some Hard Questions**—Why are you amassing a large stash of cash if you do not plan to spend it down or gift it? What are you waiting for? Will your health get better with age? Probably not. If you already have enough money to be deemed "financially independent" (i.e., not dependent on a job for income), how do you want to spend your time? If you don't spend your savings, who will (i.e., heirs, charities, federal and/or state government, etc.)? Will they respect the hard work and frugality it took to build your nest egg?

- **Automate Savings Withdrawals**—If repeatedly making cash withdrawals from saving and investment accounts makes you anxious and sad, "set it and forget it." Options include purchasing a fixed annuity that pays monthly income, managed payout mutual funds that provide investors with predictable monthly payments, bond and certificate of deposit (CD) "ladders" (i.e., multiple bonds or CDs with varying maturity dates), and automatic withdrawal options on mutual funds.

- **Get Help with Spending and Saving Decisions**—Try some online calculators to reassure yourself that it is okay to spend down your money. For example, Nerd Wallet has a tool that tells how long your savings will last or if you will ever run out of money. Simply input the annual investment return, estimated tax rate, current savings, and monthly distribution. Monte Carlo calculators estimate the probability that savings will last a certain period of time—typically 30 years. Another helpful resource is a certified financial planner. If you have accumulated enough money to worry about "flipping a switch," spend a little on a few hours of a professional advisor's time.

References

Bamikole, O.O. (2013). *The Habit Persistence Hypothesis: Empirical Evidence From Jamaica*. https://www.researchgate.net/publication/267098801_The_Habit_Persistence_Hypothesis_Empirical_Evidence_from_Jamaica

Browning, C., Guo, T., Cheng, Y., & Finke, M. (2016). Spending in Retirement: Determining the Consumption Gap. *Journal of Financial Planning*, 29(2) https://www.onefpa.org/journal/Pages/FEB16-Spending-in-Retirement-Determining-the-Consumption-Gap.aspx

Finke, M., Guo, T. & Johnson, R.R. (2018, June). Grasshoppers and Ants in Retirement. *AAII Journal*, 23-24, 29 https://www.aaii.com/journal/article/grasshoppers-and-ants-in-retirement.

Half of Retirees Afraid to Use Savings (2019). *Squared Away Blog*. Boston: Center for Retirement Research at Boston College https://squaredawayblog.bc.edu/squared-away/half-of-retirees-afraid-to-use-savings/

How Long Your Retirement Savings Will Last- And How to Stretch It (2018). *NerdWallet* https://www.nerdwallet.com/blog/investing/how-long-will-your-retirement-savings-last/

How to Create a Laddered CD Portfolio (2019). *Investopedia* https://www.investopedia.com/articles/bonds/07/ladders.asp

Managed Payout Funds vs. Annuities: How Do They Compare? (2019). *Investopedia* https://www.investopedia.com/articles/investing/093016/managed-payout-funds-vs-annuities-how-do-they-compare.asp

Monte Carlo Retirement Calculator (2019). Retirement Simulation https://www.retirementsimulation.com/

Retirement Nest Egg Calculator (2019). *Vanguard*. https://retirementplans.vanguard.com/VGApp/pe/pubeducation/calculators/RetirementNestEggCalc.jsf

2019 RCS Fact Sheet #3 Preparing for Retirement in America (2019). Washington, DC: Employee Benefit Research Institute https://www.ebri.org/docs/default-source/rcs/2019-rcs/rcs_19-fs-3_prep.pdf?sfvrsn=3a553f2f_4

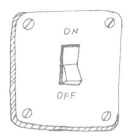

Chapter 2: Deciding When You Have "Enough"

This is another chapter that needs to acknowledge perspectives from a place of privilege. Many older adults will never get to the point of deciding whether they have enough money saved to sustain themselves in later life. Instead, they will struggle for decades to juggle expenses and make ends meet. Almost half (45 percent) of baby boomers have no savings whatsoever according to a 2019 report by the Insured Retirement Institute (IRI). Not surprisingly, one-third said they plan to exit the labor force at age 70 or beyond, or not at all. Even more sobering, the Social Security Administration estimates that 21 percent and 44 percent of married and single older adults, respectively, rely on Social Security benefits for 90 percent or more of their income. Back in 1935 when the program was created, Social Security was never meant to be a sole source of income but, rather, a base to build on with personal savings. In 2020, the average monthly Social Security benefit was $1,503 ($18,036) for the year, hardly enough money to cover living costs for most older adults.

Conscientious and consistent savers (a.k.a., "ants") are fortunate, however, to eventually get to a place where they have enough money to sustain themselves without income from an employer or dependence on other people, such as a parent. In other words, they can shift from working to make money to having their money work for them. Their "financial house" gets built and their wealth supports their lifestyle. Many people call this exalted stage of life "financial independence" or "FI" as reflected in the first two letters of the acronym FIRE (Financial Independence, Retire Early). This is the goal of a small but visible cadre of young adults who want to achieve FI by middle age and then be free to fit work into their lives if and when they want to. In 2019, *Playing with FIRE*, a documentary film about the FIRE movement, was released. It describes strategies used by its proponents to live frugally and save aggressively. A key point made about FIRE in the film is "people have figured out that, if you save half your income, you can move that retirement date from 50 years out to 17 years out." Several people profiled in the film indeed achieved FI before age 40.

Whether "ants" are following a traditional path to FI in their 50s or 60s or the "fast track" FIRE path in their 30s or 40s, they eventually come to a point of determining whether they have enough money saved to officially declare themselves financially independent. However, knowing that you have achieved FI and acting upon this information are two different things. Many super-savers find it emotionally difficult to leave their jobs. They may be ready financially but feel strong attachments to their job responsibilities, co-workers, and/or rising 401(k) balance. An article in the *Journal of Financial Planning* described the situation where people who succeed at saving more than enough money for their later years can't wrap their head around the fact that they have indeed crossed the "finish line." They continue to work because working, to them, is not all about the money. Every two or three years, they tell their financial planner that they will retire in two to three years. The article suggests that advisors set up an "as-if" investment portfolio and organize these clients' assets as if earned income has already stopped or decreased. In other words, the portfolio transitions to "retirement mode" while clients continue to work and address their mental roadblocks.

So how much money is enough to flip the switch from full-time work to part-time, occasional, or no work? The short answer is: it depends. Key factors to consider include anticipated living expenses, benefits from a previous employer (e.g., a pension and health insurance), investment asset allocation, health status, and life-expectancy projections. Several retirement savings calculators are described below. A commonly used metric that is popular with the FIRE community is saving an amount equal to 25 times annual living expenses (not income) before permanently leaving the workforce. For example, $1.25 million is 25 times $50,000 of spending, and $2.5 million is 25 times $100,000. Others have suggested 40 to 50 times expenses (and/or annual withdrawals less than the commonly recommended 4 percent of invested assets, adjusted annually for inflation) as a goal for those who achieve FI in middle age. Why? Their savings may have to last five or six decades rather than the standard 30-year timeframe that portfolio longevity research is generally based upon.

- **Do Some Savings Calculations**—Try several online calculators to determine how much money you need to save to comfortably retire. If the results say that you don't need to save any more money, you have enough. A useful tool is the interactive FINRA Retirement Calculator (https://tools.finra.org/retirement_calculator/) from the Financial Industry Regulatory Authority, a self-regulatory organization that oversees U.S. broker-dealers. Answer 13 questions about your current retirement savings, savings goal, current age, retirement age, tax rate, assumed investment return, and other personal factors, and the calculator will tell you how much you need to invest annually to meet your retirement income goal. If you are already saving enough money, the calculator will tell you that you are on track to meet your savings goal. Another way to determine if your savings is adequate is to multiply your annual spending by 25 or more.

- **Try a Monte Carlo Calculator**—Instead of calculating a specific dollar amount to save, Monte Carlo calculators use historical investment returns to indicate the probability that savings will last long enough that people will not run out of money during their remaining lifetime. Key variables in a simulation are age at retirement, amount of money saved, amount of money needed, life expectancy, and investment returns. Many financial planners use Monte Carlo software with their clients, but calculators can also be found online. Examples include calculators from Portfolio Visualizer (https://www.portfoliovisualizer.com/monte-carlo-simulation) and Vanguard (https://retirementplans.vanguard.com/VGApp/pe/pubeducation/calculators/RetirementNestEggCalc.jsf).

- **Hire a Certified Financial Planner**—Financial planners have Monte Carlo software and other tools to determine if you have saved enough. They also have training and experience to help their clients overcome behavioral biases. An example is earning $200,000 and operating with a scarcity mindset as if you still earned $40,000. The IRI study, introduced above, found that baby boomers with financial advisors were two to three times more likely to believe they did an effective job planning for retirement and their income will last throughout their lifetime. To find a local CFP ®, visit www.letsmakeaplan.org.

- **Confront Your Mental Roadblocks**—Even when you have saved enough money, leaving the workforce and adapting to a new lifestyle is scary. Like graduating from college, leaving a long career triggers feelings of anxiety, confusion, and uncertainty about the future. Psychotherapist Connie Zweig noted that "crossing the threshold into retirement can feel like a high-wire act without a net." Like Zweig, my images of the "R word" were not very positive: endless BINGO and Bunko games, ageism, and irrelevance. Like Zweig, "they're what stopped me from stopping." So, I consciously decided that my later life would not be a life without work. I love working and, as Marie Kondo would say, "it brings me joy." I now work freelance, with this book as a kick-off project, and actively avoid using any "R word" (e.g., retired, retiree, retirement) to describe myself. Instead, I refer to current work projects or simply state that I left Rutgers University. Creating a personalized vision of retirement, very much unlike that of my parents, gave me the confidence to acknowledge that I was ready to start a new chapter.

References

Anspach, D. (2019). How to Use Monte Carlo Simulations to Stress Test Your Retirement Plan. *The Balance* https://www.thebalance.com/stress-test-retirement-income-plan-2388487

Berger, R. (2017). The 25x Rule to Early Retirement. *Forbes* https://www.forbes.com/sites/robertberger/2017/02/23/the-25x-rule-to-early-retirement/#2feb57256faf

Boomer Expectations for Retirement 2019 (2019). Washington, DC: Insured Retirement Institute https://www.myirionline.org/docs/default-source/default-document-library/iri_babyboomers_whitepaper_2019_final.pdf?sfvrsn=0

Guyton, J. (2019) Overcome Behavioral Biases with the "As-If Retirement). *Journal of Financial Planning* https://www.onefpa.org/journal/Pages/AUG19-Overcome-Behavioral-Biases-with-the-As-If-Retirement.aspx

Lake, R. (2019). How to Have a Comfortable Retirement on Social Security Alone. *Investopedia.* https://www.investopedia.com/articles/retirement/011317/how-have-comfortable-retirement-social-security-alone.asp

Malito, A. (2019). How Do Super Savers Know When They Can Quit Their Jobs? *Marketwatch* https://www.marketwatch.com/story/how-do-super-savers-know-when-they-can-quit-their-jobs-2019-10-09

McSteen, M. *Fifty Years of Social Security* (n.d.). Washington, DC: Social Security Administration https://www.ssa.gov/history/50mm2.html

Playing with FIRE (2019). https://www.playingwithfire.co/the-documentary

2019 Social Security Changes (2019). Washington, DC: Social Security Administration https://www.ssa.gov/news/press/factsheets/colafacts2019.pdf

What Does Becoming Financially Independent Mean? (2019). https://womenwhomoney.com/what-does-financially-independent-mean/

Zweig, C. (2019). To Retire or Not to Retire? *Next Avenue* https://www.nextavenue.org/whether-to-retire/

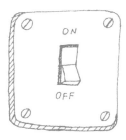

Chapter 3: Creating a "Paycheck"

Transitions and flipped switches are life events that require lasting changes in attitude and behavior. In other words, they're major shifts from one state or condition to another. One of the biggest transitions people face after they stop working is losing a steady weekly, bi-weekly, or monthly paycheck. As a result, there is a need to create a simulated "paycheck" from savings and other sources (e.g., rental property) to keep receiving income on a regular basis. Having regular streams of income throughout later life makes it easy to pay monthly household expenses, provides peace of mind, and continues a money management system that most people have practiced for decades.

The most frequently cited concern of retirees and those planning to retire soon is running out of money in later life. A 2019 survey by the American Institute of CPAs (AICPA) found that running out of money, maintaining their current lifestyle and spending level, and rising health care expenses topped a list of later life financial concerns. Nearly half (48 percent) of AICPA survey respondents were stressed over the prospect of outliving their money. Fortunately, another benefit of creating a retirement "paycheck," in addition to managing cash flow, is structuring a "safe" withdrawal rate that reduces the risk of outliving your assets. In 1994, a financial planner named Bill Bengen published a seminal study that found that an inflation-adjusted withdrawal rate of about 4 percent of a retiree's portfolio balance will generally last for 30 years when a portfolio consists of at least 50 percent stocks. If someone has saved $500,000, the first annual withdrawal would be $20,000 (e.g., $500,000 x .04 = $20,000).

Bengen's pioneering research led to what became known as the widely cited "4 Percent Rule." Assuming a 4 percent withdrawal rate, investors were told to divide the total of all their retirement savings by 25 to determine how much they could potentially withdraw each year (e.g., $500,000 ÷ 25 = a $20,000 annual withdrawal). Investors were also told to reduce withdrawals from stock or growth mutual funds during major market downturns and to keep three to five years of portfolio withdrawals in conservative cash-equivalent assets, such as bank savings or money market accounts, a money market mutual fund, or short-term certificates of deposit (CDs). The purpose of this large "cash stash" is to use during bear markets to avoid selling stocks at depressed prices. Over the past 25 years, dozens of researchers have tweaked Bengen's research methodology using different hypotheses, assumptions, and data sets.

Recent studies have recommended lower withdrawal percentages than 4 percent due to a sustained period of low interest rates on fixed income securities. A 2013 study concluded that "the 4 percent rule cannot be treated as a safe withdrawal rate in today's low interest rate environment." The researchers found a significant reduction in "safe" initial withdrawal rates, with a 4 percent initial withdrawal rate having approximately a 50 percent probability of success (i.e., not outliving one's assets) over a 30-year period. Investors who want a 90 percent probability of not outliving their assets with a 30-year time horizon and a 40 percent equity portfolio should only have an initial withdrawal rate of 2.8 percent of savings. With a $500,000 portfolio, this would equal $14,000 ($500,000 x .028) vs. $20,000 with a 4 percent withdrawal rate. A lower withdrawal rate also requires 43 percent more savings to withdraw the same amount of money from a portfolio annually as someone would get with a 4 percent withdrawal rate from a smaller portfolio. Unfortunately, many investors and even some financial advisors do not know that the former "4 Percent Rule" is no longer supported by next generation empirical research.

So, how does someone simulate a paycheck? Use strategies to arrange regular income deposits at regular time intervals. Some common retirement "paycheck" planning methods are listed below.

- **Do Some Math**—Follow the guidance from recent portfolio longevity research and amend the "4 Percent Rule." Otherwise, you could have a 50/50 chance of running out of money. Instead, consider using 2.8 percent or 3 percent of your accumulated savings as a target amount to withdraw annually. With a $1 million nest egg that many "ants" achieve after decades of savings, this would be an annual income of $28,000 or $30,000 ($2,333 to $2,500 monthly).

- **Set Up Automatic Withdrawal Plans**—Available through mutual funds, this feature allows investors to designate a dollar amount and a date (e.g., $500 on the 15th of the month) to receive an income deposit from their account. Payments are deposited directly into an investor's bank account and are made by the investment company until the account balance is depleted.

- **Consider a Managed Payout Mutual Fund**—These are a type of actively managed mutual fund, with a choice of maturity dates (e.g., 2050) that investors select to match their projected life expectancy. Payouts are structured according to the target date. The funds pay a monthly income that is generally adjusted annually for inflation and monthly payments continue until assets are exhausted.

- **Create a Bond or Certificate of Deposit (CD) "Ladder"**—A "ladder" is a portfolio of bonds or CDs with different maturities. As each bond or CD matures, the proceeds are reinvested at the longest time interval to maintain the ladder. Laddering hedges the risk of locking in a low interest rate on a large sum of money just before interest rates rise. Instead, a portion of principal is freed up on a regular basis to reinvest. Laddering can also set up a regular income stream. For example, if bonds are bought once a month for six months, investors receive monthly semi-annual interest payments, so income is received monthly.

- **Earn Some Income**—Earnings in later life provide an actual paycheck, not just a simulated one. This can help make up for decades of less-than-stellar savings. The Consumer Financial Protection Bureau found that 62 percent of workers age 55 to 64 have accumulated less than one year's worth of income in retirement savings. A $15,000 income is the equivalent of 3 percent of a $500,000 portfolio! Remaining employed also provides an opportunity to contribute to tax-deferred savings accounts and earn a higher Social Security benefit. NARFE, an organization representing federal government workers and retirees, suggested the following flexible work options: substitute teaching, child and elder care, hosting an Airbnb, mentoring, freelance writing, real estate sales, and driving for a ride-hailing company.

- **Purchase an Annuity**—Annuities are a contract with an insurance company where an investor deposits a sum of money and the insurance company makes regular payments for the investor's life (or a joint life expectancy with a spouse) or for a fixed time period. Not only do annuities provide a source of regular monthly income, but, with guaranteed income for life, they are also a longevity hedge. Annuity payments are generally based on factors such as age and gender. Investors should shop around for annuities with low expenses that are sold by insurance companies with high ratings for financial stability.

- **Tap Home Equity**—There are three common ways to turn equity into income. The first is to sell a house and move to a smaller house and/or less expensive area of the country. Profit from the sale becomes an asset to turn into income. The second strategy is a reverse mortgage that provides equity-based income as a line of credit, one-time lump sum, or regular periodic payments. The third method is a sale-leaseback arrangement. You sell your home to a close friend or family member, use the profit as a source of income, and rent the house back so you can remain in your home.

References

Bengen, W.P. (1994). Determining Withdrawal Rates Using Historical Data. *Journal of Financial Planning* http://www.retailinvestor.org/pdf/Bengen1.pdf

Blanchett, D.M., Finke, M., & Pfau, W.D. (2013). Low Bond Yields and Safe Portfolio Withdrawal Rates. *The Journal of Wealth Management*, 16(2), 55-62 https://jwm.pm-research.com/content/16/2/55.abstract

Chasen, E.A. (2019). Part-Time Work After Retirement. *NARFE*, 95(5), 24-30 https://issuu.com/narfe/docs/narfe052019

Consumer Insights on Managing Funds at the Time of Retirement (2017). Washington, DC: Consumer Financial Protection Bureau https://www.consumerfinance.gov/data-research/research-reports/consumer-insights-managing-funds-retirement/

Dixon, A. (2019). How CD Laddering Can Help Boost Your Earnings. *Bankrate* https://www.bankrate.com/banking/cds/cd-ladder-guide/

Finke, M., Pfau, W.D., & Blanchett, D. The 4 Percent Rule is Not Safe in a Low-Yield World. *SSRN* https://papers.ssrn.com/sol3/papers.cfm?abstract_id=2201323

Going Broke Remains Top Concern in Retirement: Survey of CPA Financial Planners (2019). American Institute of CPAs. https://www.aicpa.org/press/pressreleases/2019/going-broke-remains-top-concern-in-retirement.html

Managed Payout Funds vs. Annuities: How Do They Compare? (2019). *Investopedia*. https://www.investopedia.com/articles/investing/093016/managed-payout-funds-vs-annuities-how-do-they-compare.asp

Transition (2019). *Dictionary.com*. https://www.dictionary.com/browse/transition

Walser, R. (2018). *Wealth Unbroken*. Ocala, FL: Atlantic Publishing, Inc.

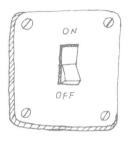

Chapter 4: RMDs: The Mandatory Flipped Switch

Most "flipped switches" involve choices. For example, after ending a long-time career, you can choose to remain employed (or self-employed), volunteer for non-profit organizations, look after your grandchildren while their parents work, move somewhere new, downsize possessions, and step up your daily physical activity...or not. There is one transition, however, where there is *no* choice. Period. It is the transition from making deposits into tax-deferred savings plans to taking annual withdrawals called required minimum distributions (RMDs) starting at age 72 (starting in 2020; formerly, the age that triggered RMDs was 70 ½).

If you are age 72 or above, getting close to that age, or are a caregiver for someone of that age, read the details below carefully to learn what you need to know.

There are two key dates to be aware of regarding RMDs: December 31 (deadline for each year's routine annual RMD withdrawals after age 72) and April 1 (deadline for postponed initial RMD withdrawals). Owners of tax-deferred accounts must begin RMDs upon reaching age 72. Some people need the money and elect to take penalty-free withdrawals as soon as they are able to starting at age 59 ½. However, financial advisors often recommend waiting to tap tax-deferred savings accounts until RMDs are required. This enables you to earn an extra decade of compound interest on your savings free of taxes, which has the effect of stretching out assets and making them last longer.

Roth IRAs, however, do not have a RMD requirement. RMD withdrawals from traditional IRAs must begin by April 1 of the year following the one in which an account owner turns 72. For example, if someone turns 72 in 2020, they have until April 1, 2021 to make their first RMD withdrawal. The downside to postponing the initial RMD withdrawal to the following year is the need to take *two* RMD withdrawals (previous year's withdrawal and current year's withdrawal) that year, which could wind up increasing your marginal tax bracket (and tax bill). After the first year, RMD withdrawals must be made by December 31 of each year. RMDs from employer savings plans, such as 401(k)s, are due when someone turns 72 or the year the employee retires, whichever comes later. This "Still Working Exception" applies only to a current employer's savings plan, however, and not to IRAs or tax-deferred plans from previous employers.

To calculate your RMD, take the balance in a tax-deferred account on December 31 of the previous year and divide it by the appropriate divisor for your age. The following IRS table provides the correct divisor for each age. You can always withdraw *more* than the required RMD amount but, of course, the money is taxed as ordinary income. Your plan custodian will send you (and the IRS) a 5498 form describing your year-end account balance. It is very important to get the RMD calculation correct. If not, the IRS charges a penalty equal to half the remaining amount that should have been taken out. For example, if the correct RMD is $10,000 and you only withdraw $5,000, you'll owe a tax penalty of $2,500 (half of $5,000).

You can combine multiple IRA accounts or multiple 403(b) accounts and take a distribution for all of them from one or any combination of accounts. You cannot, however, combine withdrawals for IRAs with other types of accounts, such as 403(b) or 401(k) plans. Withdrawals from multiple 401(k) plans must also be taken separately and cannot be combined.

Required Minimum Distribution Table

Age	Distribution Period	Age	Distribution Period
70	27.4	93	9.6
71	26.5	94	9.1
72	25.6	95	8.6
73	24.7	96	8.1
74	23.8	97	7.6
75	22.9	98	7.1
76	22.0	99	6.7
77	21.2	100	6.3
78	20.3	101	5.9
79	19.5	102	5.5
80	18.7	103	5.2
81	17.9	104	4.9
82	17.1	105	4.5
83	16.3	106	4.2
84	15.5	107	3.9
85	14.8	108	3.7
86	14.1	109	3.4
87	13.4	110	3.1
88	12.7	111	2.9
89	12.0	112	2.6
90	11.4	113	2.4
91	10.8	114	2.1
92	10.2	115+	1.9

Source: IRA Required Minimum Distribution Worksheet https://www.irs.gov/pub/irs-tege/uniform_rmd_wksht.pdf

There are three steps to calculating an accurate RMD withdrawal:

1. Review form 5498 to determine the tax-deferred account balance on December 31 of the previous year.

2. Determine the applicable divisor that corresponds with the distribution period for your age (as shown in the previous chart).

3. Divide the distribution period factor (based on life expectancy) into the reported account balance.

Consider someone with a $500,000 account balance. At age 72, the distribution divisor is 25.6., The RMD is $19,531 ($500,000 ÷ 25.6), which results in a tax bill of $4,297 and $4,687, respectively, in the 22 percent and 24 percent marginal tax brackets. RMDs as a percentage of assets resemble a big wave (a.k.a., "silver tsunami"). They are 3.9 percent of assets at age 72 (100 ÷ 25.6), but 4.4 percent (100 ÷ 22.9), 5.3 percent (100 ÷ 18.7), 8.8 percent (100 ÷ 11.4), and 15.9 (100 ÷ 6.3) percent at ages 75, 80, 90, and 100, respectively.

People who take RMD withdrawals often wonder what to do with the money. Many are "ants" who are so used to saving in tax-deferred plans that spending the money seems scary and foreign. The answer is that you can do whatever you want. Three basic options are: spend the money on living expenses, re-save the money (minus what you will owe in income tax payments) in a taxable investment account or Roth IRA (if qualified), or gift the money to people or charities. The money is yours to do with what you will, and the rest of this book can help you think through various options and reverse that "ant" mindset. Be sure to adjust your tax withholding for RMD withdrawals using quarterly estimated tax payments to the IRS or tax withholding by a savings plan custodian.

- **Learn the Law**—The best source of information about RMDs is IRS Publication 590-B, which can be downloaded from the IRS web site (www.irs.gov). It contains detailed instructions, distribution period tables based on life expectancy, and worksheets. Many banks and brokerage firms also have helpful information about RMDs to help their clients for whom they are tax-deferred savings account custodians.

- **Get Help When Needed**—The *Required Minimum Distribution Calculator* from the U.S. Securities and Exchange Commission (see link below) will show you how much you must withdraw from tax-deferred accounts starting at age 72. If you need help reporting a RMD on an income tax return, consult a CPA, enrolled agent, or other professional tax preparer. If you need help investing or gifting money that is withdrawn, consult a certified financial planner® (CFP®). To find a local CFP®, visit https://www.letsmakeaplan.org.

- **Develop a RMD Spending Plan**—IRAs and 401(k)s have been around for decades. Therefore, RMDs for super-savers are likely to run in the tens of thousands of dollars per year. For example, the initial RMD at age 72 on an account balance of $1.5 million is $58,594 ($1,500,000 ÷ 25.6) resulting in income taxes of $12,891 and $14,062, respectively, in the 22 percent and 24 percent tax brackets. Set aside funds for taxes and decide what to do with the remainder of the money. Again, there are three options: spend it, resave it, or gift it.

- **Consider a Qualified Charitable Distribution (QCD)**—A QCD is a charitable donation made with a RMD withdrawal from a traditional IRA. Withdrawals made directly to a qualified charity are excluded from taxpayers' taxable income and satisfy an IRA account owner's RMD.

Contact the IRA custodian by November, at the latest, to coordinate RMD withdrawals and QCD donations before year-end.

- **Minimize RMD Damage**—In addition to using QCDs to make charitable gifts, consider converting traditional IRA balances to a Roth IRA before age 72. Other tax-savings strategies recommended by tax attorney Rebecca Walser in her book *Wealth Unbroken* to "decide your tax bracket" are purchasing life insurance policies to preserve wealth and purchasing income annuities.

As a result of the Coronavirus Aid, Relief, and Economic Security (CARES) Act designed to address economic damage resulting from the COVID-19 global pandemic, required minimum distributions (RMDs) were suspended during 2020. This provision applied to traditional IRAs, SEP and SIMPLE IRAs, and tax-deferred employer retirement savings plans such as 401(k), 403(b), and government worker plans. The CARES Act eliminated RMDs for 2020 and RMDs that needed to be taken in 2020 by people who turned 70 ½ in 2019 and did not take their first RMD in 2019.

References

Benz, C. (2019). *Your RMD Amounts Are More Conservative Than You Might Think*. Morningstar. https://www.morningstar.com/articles/917708/your-rmd-amounts-are-more-conservative-than-you-might-think

Don't forget to take RMDs by Year-End (2019). Fidelity https://www.fidelity.com/viewpoints/retirement/december-rmd-deadline

Estimate Your Required Minimum Distributions in Retirement (2019). Vanguard https://personal.vanguard.com/us/insights/retirement/estimate-your-rmd-tool

IRA Required Minimum Distributions Table (2019). Bankrate https://www.bankrate.com/finance/money-guides/ira-minimum-distributions-table.aspx

IRA Required Minimum Distribution Worksheet. Internal Revenue Service https://www.irs.gov/pub/irs-tege/uniform_rmd_wksht.pdf

IRS Uniform Lifetime Table. Fidelity Investments https://www.fidelity.com/bin-public/060_www_fidelity_com/documents/UniformLifetimeTable.pdf

Levine, J. (2020). *Analyzing the CARES Act: From Rebate Checks to Small Business Relief for the Coronavirus Pandemic*. Kitces.com. https://www.kitces.com/blog/analyzing-the-cares-act-from-rebate-checks-to-small-business-relief-for-the-coronavirus-pandemic/

Publication 590-B; Distributions from Individual Retirement Arrangements (2018). Internal Revenue Service https://www.irs.gov/pub/irs-pdf/p590b.pdf

Required Minimum Distribution Calculator. U.S. Securities and Exchange Commission https://www.investor.gov/additional-resources/free-financial-planning-tools/required-minimum-distribution-calculator

RMD Comparison Chart (2019). Internal Revenue Service. https://www.irs.gov/retirement-plans/rmd-comparison-chart-iras-vs-defined-contribution-plans

RMD Info to IRS from Custodians (2016). Ed Slott and Company, LLC https://www.irahelp.com/forum-post/27907-rmd-info-irs-custodians

Strategies for Unneeded RMDs (2017). AAII Journal https://www.aaii.com/journal/article/strategies-for-unneeded-rmds

Walser, R. (2018). *Wealth Unbroken*. Ocala, FL: Atlantic Publishing, Inc.

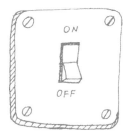

Chapter 5: Later Life Investing

Another common financial "flipped switch" is investors changing their asset allocation and becoming more conservative as they get older. Asset allocation is the process of dividing an investment portfolio (i.e., the sum total of a person's investments, whatever the amount), percentage wise, into different asset classes. For example, 50 percent stock, 30 percent bonds, and 20 percent cash equivalent assets, such as money market funds and certificates of deposit (CDs). Different investments are then purchased within each asset class.

Investment asset allocation is like a teacher's grade book where various exams and assignments are worth a certain percentage of a student's grade and are averaged together based on their percentage of the total grade. I did this with my Personal Finance class using an Excel spreadsheet. The weighted average on an investment portfolio reflects both the rate of return earned on individual investments within different asset classes (e.g., stock) and their proportionate weight (e.g., 40 percent) in the total portfolio.

Aggressive investors hold more stock in their portfolio than moderate investors, and moderate investors hold more stock than conservative investors. A frequently cited asset allocation guideline is "110 – your age" as the percentage of a portfolio to hold in stocks. For example, 110 – 50 (age) equals a 60 percent stock allocation. At age 70, the stock allocation is 40 percent (110 – 70). This declining stock glide path guideline corresponds with recommendations to gradually decrease the percentage of stocks as investors get older and shift to more income-oriented investments and because there are fewer years of life left to recover from stock market downturns.

Of course, an individual's risk tolerance also needs to be considered when determining asset class weightings at any age. Investment risk tolerance can be defined as the amount of volatility (i.e., change in the value of an investment) that an individual is willing to withstand, particularly on the downside (i.e., loss of money). This is sometimes referred to as an individual's "sleep at night factor"—how much investment risk are people willing to take before they are kept awake at night worrying about the status of their investments? Like values and goals, investment risk tolerance varies among individuals, and there is no "right" or "wrong" risk tolerance level. To score your personal investment risk tolerance using an empirically tested investment risk tolerance assessment tool, see http://pfp.missouri.edu/research_IRTA.html 280.

Not everyone agrees with the "110 – your age" rule or its cousins "100 – your age" (for conservative investors) and "120 – your age" (for aggressive investors). One reason is a belief that people should select securities based on their risk tolerance, investment objectives, and available resources. Another reason for this is because of findings from recent research. A study by Kitces and Pfau found that the "100 – your age" asset allocation delivered the worst outcome among various asset allocation methods in a poor stock market. When retirements began in overvalued stock markets, a rising equity glide path (i.e., more stock as investors got older) showed potential to provide downside risk protection. A static 60 percent stock allocation was also found to be "nearly optimal" in most investment market situations. A key take-away is to create an asset allocation plan that works in worst-case scenarios because stock market returns are unpredictable. The "100 – your age" formula is not the best allocation approach to use because it does not fare well under poor stock market conditions.

Another fact about later life investing is that older adults are frequent victims of investment fraud. They have more money than younger investors, are home more frequently, and may be experiencing social isolation or diminished mental capacity. The movies *Boiler Room* and *The Wolf of Wall Street* provide valuable insights into how unscrupulous operators can steal victims' money by peddling worthless or nonexistent securities.

Older investors, therefore, need to flip another investment-related switch and raise their "BS meter," so to speak. How can you tell if an investment is fraudulent? Below are four "red flags" to look out for:

- **Future Predictions**—Beware of marketers that *guarantee* an investment's future return. With the exception of bonds, investment returns will always be unpredictable to a certain degree, and the value of securities rises and falls with market trends.

- **Quick Cash**—Beware of scam artists who promise *fast, low-risk* payoffs and compare their returns to low rates available on bank accounts or bonds. Their implication is that victims are "suckers" for settling for low returns and that they have a sure, *guaranteed* path to high returns in a short period of time.

- **Lack of Information**—Beware of background information about fraudulent investments that is misleading, vague, or not provided at all. These marketers do not want to give consumers the ability to assess their claims. Request a company's financial statements. If you are not able to access this information, this is a major red flag.

- **Immediate Response**—Beware of scam artists who require an *immediate response* and/or *an immediate deposit of funds*. Urgency is important to swindlers, so they get their victims' money before they have time to second-guess their decisions or contact others for advice.

Information is an investor's best tool when it comes to investing wisely and avoiding fraud and scams. The best way to gather information is to ask detailed questions about the potential investment and the person or firm selling it. Think twice and seek out advice, should you desire, *before* investing money in or committing yourself to any opportunity you learn about online. It is very easy for swindlers to make their messages look real and credible. Always remember: if something sounds too good to be true, it probably is!

- **Assess Yourself as an Investor**—Use an online asset allocation calculator to determine your current asset allocation weightings. Then take several investment risk tolerance assessments to determine your appetite for investment risk. Some tools ask people about investment decisions they made in the past, some ask them to respond to hypothetical scenarios that involve investment risk, and some do both.

- **Tweak the "110 – Your Age" Formula**—Key factors to consider are your risk tolerance, investment goals, and research results. A balanced portfolio with 60 percent stock and 40 percent fixed-income securities was found to work well under varying market conditions. Another option is a target-date fund with a "through retirement" asset allocation that is aligned with its investors' age.

- **Rebalance Regularly**—The asset allocation percentages of your portfolio will shift over time according to stock and bond market performance. Rebalance your portfolio periodically to get back to your original asset allocation weights. Rebalancing can be done by selling securities in an over-weighted asset class (e.g., stocks after a bull market) or putting new investment dollars into an under-weighted asset class.

- **Beware of "Free Meal" Seminars**—These seminars are designed to solicit older investors, often with promises of "guaranteed" income and attractive returns. There is often a "hard sell" at the seminar or afterwards. State securities regulators have prosecuted a variety of violations stemming from these events, including the sale of unsuitable investment products and misrepresentation of investment returns and advisor credentials.

References

Asset Allocation Calculator (2019). Sentinel Benefits and Financial Group. https://www.sentinelgroup.com/Individuals/Resources/Calculators/Asset-Allocation-Calculator

Beginners' Guide to Asset Allocation, Diversification, and Rebalancing (2010). U.S. Securities and Exchange Commission. https://www.investor.gov/sites/investorgov/files/2019-02/Beginners-Guide-to-Asset-Allocation.pdf

Investment Risk Tolerance Assessment (2019). University of Missouri http://pfp.missouri.edu/research_IRTA.html

Investor Alert for Seniors: Five Red Flags of Investment Fraud (2017). U.S. Securities and Exchange Commission. https://www.sec.gov/oiea/investor-alerts-bulletins/ia_5redflags.html

Kitces, M.E., & Pfau, W.D. (2015). Retirement Risk, Rising Equity Glide Paths, and Valuation-Based Asset Allocation. *Journal of Financial Planning* https://www.onefpa.org/journal/Documents/March2015_Contribution_Kitces.pdf

Red Flags of Fraud (2019). FINRA https://www.finra.org/investors/red-flags-fraud

Senior Investor Alert: Free Meal Seminars (2019), NASAA https://www.nasaa.org/1950/senior-investor-alert-free-meal-seminars/

Stock Allocation Rules. *Investopedia* https://www.investopedia.com/articles/investing/062714/100-minus-your-age-outdated.asp

The "100 Minus Age" Rule Puts Retirees at Risk (2019). *The Balance* https://www.thebalance.com/100-minus-age-allocation-approach-puts-retirees-at-risk-2388296

Updegrave, W. (2013). Investing Rules of Thumb: Why They Don't Always Work. *Money* http://money.com/money/2793758/investing-rules-of-thumb-why-they-dont-always-work/

What's the best asset allocation for my age? (2018). CNN Money https://money.cnn.com/retirement/guide/investing_basics.moneymag/index7.htm

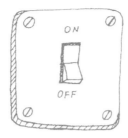

Chapter 6: Adjusting to Changes in Income and Expenses

In a number of states across the U.S., students in grades as young as kindergarten are studying the basics of personal finance. In July 2019, North Carolina became the 20th state to implement a financial literacy course requirement for high school students. A key concept taught in elementary, secondary, and college personal finance courses is cash flow management, a.k.a., budgeting. Students are taught to achieve flat or—ideally—positive cash flow, where income equals or exceeds expenses.

While considerable attention is paid to helping young adults learn to live within their means as they prepare to enter the labor force, the same cannot be said for people who are leaving long-time careers. In stark contrast to the large number of "Adulting 101" and life skills courses that exist for young adults, few places teach older adults how to be financially successful and manage their cash flow appropriately in later life.

There are only two ways that income can change after long-time paychecks end. Individuals or couples can transition from a *higher to a lower income*, as is often the case when they lack meaningful savings and/or a pension and Social Security replaces just a fraction of what they earned. Conversely, some people transition from a *lower to a higher income*, often when a combination of pension benefits, savings withdrawals, Social Security, or other income sources exceed their pre-retirement earnings. Many "ants" and higher earners fall into the latter category, which provides further evidence of a need for them to step up their spending or charitable gifting. As we discussed in Chapter 1—if you don't spend your money, someone else will!

This chapter focuses on downward lifestyle adjustments that occur for many reasons including insufficient savings, health issues, investment losses, widowhood (two benefit checks for a couple are reduced to one), divorce, and loss of public benefits. An example of a loss of public benefits is people turning 65 who "age out" of Affordable Care Act subsidies. Transitioning to Medicare and purchasing a supplemental plan can significantly increase their monthly health care outlays. A Harvard study found that people who rely heavily on Social Security for income "have little opportunity for income growth beyond cost-of-living increases." Not surprisingly, the report described a growing disparity in incomes among older adults.

Expenses that are likely to decrease or end in later life include contributions to tax-deferred employer saving plans, work-related expenses (e.g., commuting) and clothing, housing once a mortgage is repaid, and federal and state income taxes. Expenses likely to rise include life and health insurance premiums, medical expenses, leisure activities, and gifting and charitable contributions. Whether your expense decreases will offset your expense increases is subjective based on your personal circumstances. According to AARP columnist Jean Chatzky, five budget busters after age 65 are future price increases due to inflation, outsized generosity to children and grandchildren, keeping up with spending by friends, sickness, and longevity.

When expenses exceed income, people respond by spending down savings, borrowing money, or doing without. Understandably, running out of money is one of the biggest fears of older adults. Research by Allianz Life found that more than 60 percent of baby boomers are more afraid of running out of money during their lifetime than they are of dying. The Employee Benefit Research Institute (EBRI) confirmed that these fears are not unfounded. According to research by EBRI, 83 percent of baby boomers in the lowest income quartile, 47 percent of boomers in the second-lowest quartile, 28 percent of boomers in the second-highest quartile, and 13 percent of boomers in the highest income quartile are projected to run out of money in retirement.

What can be done to prevent this? There are two basic courses of action that can be taken to help yourself adjust to changes in income and expenses: save more before leaving a long-term career and/or spend less afterward. Below are nine catch-up strategies to close the gap between available income and anticipated expenses.

- **Invest More Aggressively**—Increase the percentage of your investments held in stock or stock mutual funds. You will take on more risk but will also have the potential for a higher long-term return versus cash assets and bonds. With a higher return, savings will last longer.

- **Work Longer**—Remain on the job longer than you may have originally planned. Even just one or two more years of work can make a big difference. That's one or two more years to save in tax-deferred plans, higher pension and/or Social Security benefits, and one or two fewer years you'll have to withdraw from your savings accounts for income. One study found that a 66-year-old worker who works one year longer and puts off claiming Social Security for one year longer receives a 7.75 percent increase in inflation-adjusted income, with 83 percent of this amount coming from higher Social Security benefits.

- **Trade Down to a Smaller Home**—Consider moving to a smaller living space for reasons that include lower maintenance, utility bills, and/or property taxes. Taking this step will probably require downsizing in other areas as well, so plan early to pare down possessions via trash disposal, recycling, and/or gifts to family members and charities.

- **Geographic Arbitrage**—Consider moving to another area of your state or the country where you do not have to downsize but will still have lower living costs and property taxes. Take for example, a relocation from high-tax New York City to a rural area of Florida, where there is no state income tax. A major disadvantage of this strategy is moving away from familiar people and places.

- **Continue Working**—Consider some type of paid employment or self-employment to supplement Social Security and other income sources. Earnings will reduce the amount of savings required. For example, $20,000 of earnings is equivalent to 4 percent of a $500,000 portfolio and $40,000 is equivalent to 4 percent of $1 million. Beware, however, of the Social Security earnings limit. See Chapter 8 for details.

- **Tap Home Equity**—Consider ways to convert equity in your home into a stream of income. A strategy used by some older adults is applying for a reverse mortgage to receive a lump sum, monthly payments, or a line of credit. A second strategy, known as sale-leaseback, is selling your home to a close friend or relative who rents it back to you, so you can stay in your home.

- **Spend Less**—Prepare a budget for your anticipated post-employment income. Decide what percentage of previous income is necessary (e.g., 70 percent). Identify expense categories that can be trimmed, if necessary. It is also not uncommon for expense reduction to occur naturally, as older adults realize they have "enough" of certain items such as clothing and home furnishings.

- **Make Tax-Efficient Asset Withdrawals**—For some (but not all) people, it makes sense to withdraw money first from taxable accounts, then tax-deferred accounts, and then tax-free accounts and Roth IRAs to allow tax-advantaged funds to grow as long as possible. Another withdrawal strategy that is increasingly being recommended is the "proportional method," where investors withdraw assets from all three types of accounts (taxable, tax-deferred, and tax-free) each year in proportion to their portfolio weighting.

- **Access Public Benefits**—Unfortunately, many people with a middle-class lifestyle during their working years end up in poverty. According to a 2018 study by the New School, roughly 40 percent of Americans who are considered middle class (based on their income levels) will fall into poverty or near poverty by the time they reach age 65. You can assess your risk of experiencing poverty with an interactive *Poverty Risk Simulator* at https://confrontingpoverty.org/poverty-risk-calculator/. If this happens to you, reach out to local non-profit and government agencies for food pantries, rental assistance, and other aid.

References

Backman, M. (2018). *Will Your Expenses Stay the Same in Retirement?* CNN Money https://money.cnn.com/2018/05/07/retirement/expenses-in-retirement/index.html

Boomers at 80: Housing Issues to Grow (2019). Center for Retirement Research at Boston College. https://squaredawayblog.bc.edu/squared-away/boomers-at-80-housing-issues-to-grow/

Chatzky, J. (2018, May). Budget Busters in Retirement. *AARP The Magazine*, 26.

Coxwell, K. (2019). *What Happens If I Really Do Run Out of Money in Retirement?* New Retirement. https://www.newretirement.com/retirement/what-happens-if-i-really-do-run-out-of-money-in-retirement/

Dinkin, E. (2019). *40% of the American Middle Class Face Poverty in Retirement, Study Concludes.* CNBC. https://www.cnbc.com/2018/10/12/40percent-of-american-middle-class-face-poverty-in-retirement-study-says.html

Franklin, M. (2018). Working Longer is the Best Way to Boost Retirement Income. *Investment News.* https://www.investmentnews.com/article/20180725/BLOG05/180729954/working-longer-is-best-way-to-boost-retirement-income

Housing America's Older Adults 2019 (2019) Joint Center for Housing Studies of Harvard University. https://www.jchs.harvard.edu/housing-americas-older-adults-2019

How We Used Geographic Arbitrage to Retire 9 Years Ahead of Schedule (2018). Retire by 45. https://www.retireby45.com/how-we-used-geographic-arbitrage-to-retire-9-years-ahead-of-schedule/

Keshner, A. (2019). North Carolina is 20th State to Require Financial Literacy Class for High Schoolers. *MarketWatch* https://www.marketwatch.com/story/more-states-consider-mandatory-financial-literacy-classes-as-high-school-students-struggle-with-basic-budgeting-2019-06-19

Pfau, W.D. (2016). Incorporating Home Equity into a Retirement Income Strategy. *Journal of Financial Planning* 29 (4): 41–49 https://www.onefpa.org/journal/Pages/APR16-Incorporating-Home-Equity-into-a-Retirement-Income-Strategy.aspx

Tax-Savvy Withdrawals in Retirement (2019). Fidelity Investments https://www.fidelity.com/viewpoints/retirement/tax-savvy-withdrawals

VanDerhei, J. (2014). *'Short' Falls: Who's Most Likely to Come up Short in Retirement, and When?* Employee Benefit Research Institute. https://papers.ssrn.com/sol3/papers.cfm?abstract_id=2457053

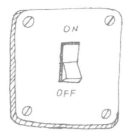

Chapter 7: Tax Withholding–It's Not What You Earn, It's What You Keep

Decades ago, the investment firm Nuveen created the slogan, "It's not what you earn, it's what you keep" to encourage investors to buy tax-free municipal bonds that provide a higher after-tax return than higher-yielding taxable bonds. This phrase can also apply to income from Social Security, pensions, annuities, tax-deferred employer savings plans, capital gains from taxable accounts, and other sources of income in later life. The difference, versus earnings from a job, is that there may not be tax withheld on these income sources. Rather, taxpayers are "on their own" to pay estimated taxes to the IRS on a timely basis.

Taxpayers are responsible for paying their tax liability throughout the year via payroll withholding and/or quarterly estimated-tax payments to the IRS. Quarterly payments may be new "switch" for people who previously received an employer paycheck with tax withholding for decades. Payments are due April 15, June 15, September 15, and January 15 of the following calendar year. Some people have difficulty completing their tax return by the tax-filing deadline, which falls on or around April 15, but can request an automatic six-month extension of time to file. For federal taxes, they would electronically file or mail a paper copy of Form 4868. All taxes due must be paid in April, however, even though an extension of time for filing is requested.

Income from pensions, annuities, and tax-deferred savings plans funded with pre-tax dollars (income that was not previously taxed) is taxable as ordinary income. Plan providers send a 1099-R form with information about how much money was disbursed from a retirement plan, such as a pension, IRA, annuity, and 401(k), and how much of it is taxable. The term "ordinary income" refers to income other than dividends and long-term capital gains from investments and includes income from salaries and wages, bonuses, commissions, tips, and self-employment.

Non-retirement account withdrawals are also taxable. When an investor sells securities and earns a profit, capital gains are realized and income tax is due. Conversely, an investment sale can also result in a capital loss. When this happens, the loss can be used to offset capital gains earned on other investments. People realize capital gains when they "buy low" (e.g., stock purchased for $10 a share) and "sell high" (e.g., stock sold for $20 a share). The difference between the amount paid for an asset initially and over time (i.e., its tax basis) and the amount for which it was sold is the capital gain. Capital gains may be short-term or long-term, depending upon an investment's holding period.

A short-term capital gain is a profit made on assets that are held for a year or less, and a long-term gain is a gain on assets held more than one year. Both types of capital gains must be claimed on tax returns, but they are taxed very differently. Short-term capital gains are taxed as ordinary income based on an investor's marginal tax rate, which is determined by tax-filing status (e.g., single, married filing jointly, head of household) and taxable income. Long-term capital gains are taxed at a lower tax rate. Long-term capital gain tax rates on 2020 federal income tax returns are 0, 15, and 20 percent, also depending on an investor's taxable income and tax filing status. Ideally, investments should be held long term to receive more favorable tax treatment. It is also wise for investors, especially those with significant assets, to monitor their tax withholding.

So how do you "flip a switch" and start making quarterly estimated tax payments? Follow these steps:

- **Calculate Estimated Income**—Make your best estimate of total income for the year and subtract expected tax deductions and tax credits. Use your prior year's tax return as a reference point for calculations, making adjustments for changes in age, income sources, and employment status.

- **Calculate Estimated Taxes**—Determine your estimated tax using IRS Form 1040-ES. Take your estimated annual tax liability and divide it by 4. Be sure to include self-employment tax, if applicable. This number is estimated net business income x .9235, then multiplied by 15.3 percent, the self-employment tax rate (12.4 percent for Social Security tax plus 2.9 percent for Medicare). Subtract tax withholding that is already being provided.

- **Calculate Quarterly Payments**—Add together estimated income tax and/or self-employment tax for the entire year and divide by four. Send payments to the IRS by the dates noted above. Take care to avoid the penalty for underpayment of estimated taxes. According to the IRS, "Generally, most taxpayers will avoid this penalty if they owe less than $1,000 in tax after subtracting their withholdings and credits, or if they paid at least 90% of tax for the current year, or 100% of tax shown on the return for the prior year, whichever is smaller."

- **Request Income Tax Withholding Services**—Check with the custodians of your pension and/or tax-deferred accounts to see if income tax withholding is available. If so, complete the necessary tax-withholding paperwork using Form W-4. This form was redesigned by the IRS in 2020  and includes five steps (two required and three optional) instead of the previous complicated worksheets and withholding allowances. Line 4a of Form W-4 includes sources of income that are not subject to withholding.

- **Determine Your New Marginal Tax Rate**—Check the table below to see if tax-deferred account withdrawals and other new income sources in later life could increase your marginal tax rate or if less income in retirement could reduce it. The 2020 tax rates for single filers and couples filing jointly are as follows:

Single Filers	Married Couples Filing Jointly
10 percent for incomes up to $9,875	10 percent for incomes up to $19,750
12 percent for incomes over $9,875	12 percent for incomes over $19,750
22 percent for incomes over $40,125	22 percent for incomes over $80,250
24 percent for incomes over $85,525	24 percent for incomes over $171,050
32 percent for incomes over $163,300	32 percent for incomes over $326,600
35 percent for incomes over $207,350	35 percent for incomes over $414,700
37 percent for incomes over $518,400	37 percent for incomes over $622,050

- **Earmark Income for Tax Withholding**—Set aside 25 to 30 percent of all income for which tax withholding is not available to make quarterly estimated tax payments. The only other way to ensure that enough tax is paid is to over-withhold income tax via an employer if you decide to continue working.

- **Time Elective Cash Withdrawals**—Time withdrawals from savings and investments that are not required by tax law (e.g., required minimum distributions). Ideally, take money out in a year when ordinary income is reduced to avoid being taxed at a higher marginal tax rate.

- **Consider Hiring a Tax Pro**—Consult a CPA, enrolled agent, or other professional tax-preparer for advice on tax withholding and to prepare taxes for at least the first tax season after leaving full-time employment. Use the professionally prepared return as a template to follow in the future.

References

Anspach, D. (2019). *Here's What to Know About Retirement Income*. https://www.thebalance.com/taxable-partially-taxable-and-tax-free-retirement-income-2388975

Caplinger, D. (2019). *How Much Tax You'll Pay on Long-Term Capital Gains in 2020*. https://www.fool.com/taxes/2019/11/09/how-much-tax-youll-pay-on-long-term-capital-gains.aspx

Estimated Taxes (2019). Internal Revenue Service. https://www.irs.gov/businesses/small-businesses-self-employed/estimated-taxes

FAQs on the Draft 2020 Form W-4 (2019). Internal Revenue Service: https://www.irs.gov/newsroom/faqs-on-the-draft-2020-form-w-4

Fishman, S. (2019). *How Many 1099 Forms Are There?* Nolo. https://www.nolo.com/legal-encyclopedia/how-many-1099-forms-are-there.html

Here's How and When to Pay Estimated Taxes. Internal Revenue Service. https://www.irs.gov/newsroom/heres-how-and-when-to-pay-estimated-taxes

Investing in America 2019. Nuveen. https://documents.nuveen.com/Documents/Nuveen/Default.aspx?uniqueId=1b3974e4-d460-4b47-845d-51cae2a071bb

IRS Releases Updated Income Tax Brackets for 2020 (2019). Fox Business. https://www.foxbusiness.com/money/income-tax-brackets-for-2020

McCool, C. (2019). *How to Calculate and Pay Estimated Taxes*. Bench. https://bench.co/blog/tax-tips/estimated-tax-payments/

New W-4 Form for 2020 Eliminates Those Confusing 'Allowances' (2019). https://www.creditkarma.com/insights/i/new-w-4-form-2020-allowances/

Ordinary Income (2019). Investopedia. https://www.investopedia.com/terms/o/ordinaryincome.asp

When to Use Tax Form 1099-R: Distributions from Pensions, Annuities, Retirement, etc. (2019). Intuit Turbo Tax. https://turbotax.intuit.com/tax-tips/retirement/when-to-use-tax-form-1099-r-distributions-from-pensions-annuities-retirement-etc/L0g2CrvvL

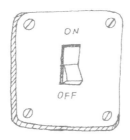

Chapter 8: Becoming a Social Security Beneficiary

One "switch" that people flip, usually once they enter their 60s, is transitioning from paying FICA tax to collecting Social Security. Workers who qualify for benefits with at least 40 calendar quarters (i.e., 10 years) of "covered work" (i.e., income on which FICA tax is charged) are eligible for benefits and can apply as early as age 62. After age 70, there is no longer any additional benefit increase for postponing filing. About 90 percent of U.S. workers (excluding some government workers, foreign nationals working in the U.S., railroad employees, and those with "underground" income) are covered.

When do most people collect Social Security? According to the Social Security Administration, the most common age by far to receive benefits is 62 (34.3 percent). Over half (57.3 percent) of beneficiaries receive benefits before reaching full retirement age (FRA): 6.3 percent at age 63, 6.4 percent at age 64, and 10.3 percent at age 65. FRA is steadily increasing and is currently age 66 (for workers born from 1943 to 1954) or age 67 (for workers born in 1960 or later) or somewhere in between (e.g., 66 and 6 months for those born in 1957). Other benefit-claiming ages are 66 (18.1 percent), 67 to 69 (3.9 percent), and 70 (3.7 percent). Eight percent a year delayed retirement credits, available between FRA and age 70, stop accruing at age 70.

The decision about when to collect Social Security affects the financial security of recipients and their surviving spouses for decades. Thus, it deserves careful scrutiny and a complete understanding of the implications of collecting early versus at FRA or later. What age is best to start receiving benefits? The SSA's official response is: "The answer is that there's not a single 'best age' for everyone and ultimately, it's your choice." Key decision-making factors include personal health status and projected life expectancy, spousal or child benefits, employment plans, income needs, and other retirement resources, such as a pension and tax-deferred investments. Some people also cite concerns about the future sustainability of Social Security with comments like, "I'm going to take it at age 62 while I still can" and "Take the money and run."

From a purely mathematical standpoint, a key factor in deciding when to receive benefits is "break-even age." This is the age, generally late 70s to early 80s (depending upon assumptions used), when someone receives more from Social Security by delaying benefits to FRA than they would by taking an early reduced benefit at age 62. Under current Social Security rules, benefits are reduced 25 percent at age 62 for persons with a FRA of 66 and 30 percent for younger workers with a FRA of 67.

Social Security benefits at various ages are designed to be about actuarially equivalent for beneficiaries with average life expectancies. Thus, they will collect roughly the same amount by claiming early benefits or waiting to collect benefits at FRA. Those with above-average life expectancies are better off, at least mathematically, waiting until FRA (or later) to collect their first check. A larger benefit will last the remainder of their life. Conversely, those who die soon after leaving work will not live long enough to reach their break-even age.

If only we had a crystal ball to tell us what to do… Unfortunately, there are no crystal balls, but there are resources to guide us. Online calculators are available by searching the words "Social Security Break-Even Calculator." To use them correctly, you'll first need to obtain a current Social Security benefit estimate from https://www.ssa.gov/myaccount/ to input data on your expected benefit at ages 62, FRA, and 70.

You can also calculate your break-even age with simple math. As an example, assume that a potential beneficiary is considering a choice between receiving $1,500 a month at FRA or $1,125 (a 25 percent permanent reduction) at age 62. An online calculator provides a break-even age of 78 years. Someone could also manually double check the math behind the calculation: $1,125 x 192 months (16 years) from age 62 to 78 equals $216,000, versus $1,500 x 144 months (12 years) from age 66 to 78, which equals $216,000. After age 78, the cumulative value of larger benefits starting at FRA will pull ahead. Those who live into their 80s, 90s, or 100s will be happy they waited until FRA.

The break-even calculation is not perfect, however. Some experts suggest adding several years to the calculated result, if someone has retirement savings, because it does not account for earnings on savings not withdrawn when early Social Security benefits are received. Some early beneficiaries may be able to leave their investments growing instead of making investment withdrawals if their Social Security benefit and, perhaps, a pension and/or part-time job is adequate.

Another factor to consider is benefit-claiming strategies for married couples, who have more options than singles because spouses can claim individual benefits at different times and may also qualify for spousal benefits. On this point, the SSA notes, "If you are the higher earner, and you delay your retirement benefit, it will result in higher monthly benefits for the rest of your life and higher survivor protection for your spouse, if you die first." A commonly recommended strategy is for lower-earning spouses to start benefits early and higher-earning spouses to delay benefits as long as possible. When one spouse dies, one Social Security check goes away, and the larger of the two remains.

- **Request a Social Security Benefit Estimate**—Check your Social Security statement annually to update expected benefits at ages 62, FRA, and 70 and to confirm that earnings information is accurate. Use the "My Account" feature of the SSA website. The SSA Retirement Estimator also provides benefit estimates based on your Social Security earnings record. See https://www.ssa.gov/benefits/retirement/estimator.html. Social Security benefits are based on a worker's highest 35 years of earnings.

- **Apply Social Security Benefit Information**—Use a tool such as the FINRA Retirement Calculator (https://tools.finra.org/retirement_calculator/) to determine savings targets for a comfortable lifestyle in later life. Perform calculations for leaving full-time employment at ages 62, FRA, and 70 and input estimated Social Security benefit amounts obtained from SSA.

- **Take Care of Your Spouse**—Consider this sobering study of Social Security benefit-claiming by the Center for Retirement Research. Using an online experiment, they found that husbands do not seem to consider the prospective drop in income experienced by their widows when choosing a benefit-claiming age. Rather, husbands responded more to concerns, such as pension incentives and health conditions, than to an information intervention that highlighted the likelihood and consequences of widowhood.

- **Make Estimated Payments for Social Security Taxes**—Send quarterly tax payments to the IRS or request income tax withholding if you owe taxes on Social Security benefits. Up to 85 percent of benefits may be taxable. Single taxpayers with an income of more than $25,000 and married couples filing jointly with a combined income of more than $32,000 must pay taxes on their benefits.

- **Beware of the Earnings Limit**—Consider your employment plans before applying for Social Security. Beneficiaries between age 62 and FRA, who earn more than $18,240 (2020 figure) before the year of their FRA, will have their benefit reduced by $1 for every $2 over the $18,240 limit. For example, if your earnings are $22,240 ($4,000 over the annual limit), the benefit amount would be reduced by $2,000 for the year. A special earnings limit rule applies for the year that workers reach their FRA. In 2020, that limit is $48,600, and workers lose $1 in annual benefits for every $3 earned over this limit until the month they reach FRA.

References

Are Some Kinds of Employees Not Covered by Social Security? AARP. https://www.aarp.org/retirement/social-security/questions-answers/kinds-of-employees-not-covered-by-social-security/

Frankel, M. (2017). *Why Do So Many People Claim Social Security at 62?* The Motley Fool. https://www.fool.com/retirement/2017/04/02/why-do-so-many-people-claim-social-security-at-62.aspx

Horton, M. (2019). *How Do I Calculate My Social Security Beak-Even Age?* Investopedia. https://www.investopedia.com/ask/answers/020615/how-do-i-calculate-my-social-security-breakeven-age.asp

Income Taxes and Your Social Security Benefits (n.d.). Social Security Administration: https://www.ssa.gov/planners/taxes.html

Konish, L. (2019). *Deciding When to Claim Social Security Based on Break-Even Calculations? Be Careful.* CNBC. https://www.cnbc.com/2019/09/09/social-security-break-even-calculations-can-be-misleading-for-retirees.html

Social Security Break-Even Calculator (2019). The Standard. https://www.standard.com/individual/retirement/planning-tools-calculators/social-security-break-even-calculator

Social Security Tips for Couples (2019). Fidelity Investments. https://www.fidelity.com/viewpoints/retirement/social-security-tips-for-couples

Social Security: The 'Break-Even' Debate (2019). Center for Retirement Research. https://squaredawayblog.bc.edu/squared-away/social-security-the-break-even-debate/

2020 Social Security Changes (2019). Social Security Administration. https://www.ssa.gov/news/press/factsheets/colafacts2020.pdf

Weston, L. (2019). *The Six Biggest Retirement Mistakes, and 1 Defense.* WTOP. https://wtop.com/lifestyle/2019/09/liz-weston-the-6-biggest-retirement-mistakes-and-1-defense/

What are Delayed Retirement Credits and How Do They Work? (2018). AARP. https://www.aarp.org/retirement/social-security/questions-answers/delayed-retirement-credits/

What's the Most Popular Age to Take Social Security? A Foolish Take (2018). The Motley Fool. https://www.fool.com/retirement/2018/06/11/a-foolish-take-whats-the-most-popular-age-to-take.aspx

When to Start Receiving Retirement Benefits (2019). Social Security Administration. https://www.ssa.gov/pubs/EN-05-10147.pdf

Who is Eligible for Social Security Retirement Benefits? (2019). Elder Law Answers. https://www.elderlawanswers.com/who-is-eligible-for-social-security-retirement-benefits-12052

Would Greater Awareness of Social Security Survivor Benefits Affect Claiming Decisions? (2018). Center for Retirement Research. http://crr.bc.edu/wp-content/uploads/2018/10/wp_2018-12.pdf

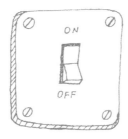

Chapter 9: Health Care Transitions

Health care transitions in later life are a virtual certainty, bringing new switches to flip. The first "switch" is the increasing cost of health care as people get older. According to the U.S. Department of Health and Human Services, average health care costs for people age 65 and over are $11,316 per year versus $2,985 for those age 18 to 44 and $6,406 for those age 45 to 64. As people age, body parts (e.g., knees and hips) wear out and health care issues (e.g., cancer, diabetes, heart conditions) surface more frequently. Even though Medicare pays for some expenses, it doesn't cover everything, resulting in substantial out-of-pocket costs for Medigap policy premiums and out-of-pocket expenses.

Fidelity Investments estimated that a 65-year-old couple in 2017 would spend an average of $275,000 of their own savings (after-tax dollars) for health care costs (excluding long-term care, dental work, vision care, and over-the-counter medicines) during the remainder of their lives. In 2018, the cost figure was $280,000, and in 2019, it was $285,000; it will likely continue to increase as a result of longer lifespans and rising costs. For single older adults, health cost estimates in 2019 were $150,000 for women and $135,000 for men. Baked into these estimates are Medicare premiums (Parts B and D); deductibles, co-payments, and co-insurance for doctor and hospital visits; and prescription drug costs. Not included were expenses that Medicare doesn't cover. According to Fidelity, which uses this data to promote tax-advantaged health savings accounts, average retirees can expect to allocate 15 percent of their annual expenses to health care costs.

If you're thinking that you will simply eat right, exercise, sleep enough, not smoke, and drink little, if any, alcohol to have "below average" health care expenses, think again. Although it sounds counterintuitive, your expenses will likely be higher. A study by the Center for Retirement Research at Boston College found that currently healthy older adults incur higher lifetime health care costs than those who are sick. How can this be? Simply put, they're around longer to incur more costs. More years of paying out-of-pocket expenses, the likelihood of developing a chronic disease later in life (compared to unhealthy people who pass away earlier in life), and a higher risk of needing long-term care by surviving to advanced old age when the risk for needing assistance with activities of daily living increases.

A second health care "switch" is the experience of buying health insurance as an individual for the first time if it has been an employee benefit for your entire career. Most people age 65 and older on Medicare purchase a supplemental health insurance (a.k.a., Medigap) policy to cover expenses that Medicare does not cover. Medigap policies are sold by private insurance companies and are standardized across insurers to facilitate comparison shopping. There are 10 available plan types with letter names, and each plan with the same letter must offer the same basic benefits. A good resource for information and counseling about Medigap (and long-term care) insurance is the State Health Insurance Assistance Program: https://www.shiptacenter.org/. In some states, this program has a different name (e.g., SHINE in Florida and South Dakota).

A third "switch" is about 2,500 hours of free time annually when people stop working and commuting to work . They have the potential to change how people manage their personal health. Studies have shown that healthy living habits improve during tough economic times. When people are unemployed, they drive less (resulting in fewer car accidents) and have more time for sleep, physical activity, and healthy meal preparation. But does the same hold true when older adults leave the workforce voluntarily? Research results are mixed. With increased leisure time, many people do practice healthier habits, but, for some, there is now more time to do unhealthful things, like drinking excessively. Illnesses and depression can also take a toll. Researchers have found that negative health effects are more common when people are forced to retire and less common when retirees have social supports and continue to work part-time.

- **Take Care of Yourself**—Take care of your body to stave off chronic diseases (e.g., diabetes) and maintain quality of life, so aging does not become painful. Many health conditions respond positively to dietary changes. Standard recommendations for older adults include eating high-fiber foods, drinking beverages fortified with Vitamin D and calcium, and drinking ample water throughout the day.

- **Start Small**—Do not let expert recommendations, like walking 10,000 steps per day, intimidate you. A 2019 study found that walking about half as many steps still has substantial health benefits. Make positive health practices automatic by turning them into habits that become part of your daily routine.

- **Earmark a Nest Egg**—Identify a portion of assets for out-of-pocket medical expenses and/or long-term care. Self-insure amounts suggested by research and current costs. For example, $290,000 for health care (Fidelity study) and $360,000 for long-term care ($10,000 per month x 36 months of care). This strategy is most often advised for households with a net worth of $1.5 to $2.5 million or more. Defined benefit pensions, annuities, and Social Security are also resources for health care because they pay lifetime benefits.

- **Work Longer**—Consider working for a few additional years before severing ties with a long-time employer. Not only will you have that many more years to save, but you can take advantage of employee health insurance (and avoid paying Part B Medicare payments) a little longer and likely qualify for a higher Social Security benefit with which to pay future health care costs.

- **Learn About Medicare**—Brush up on Medicare rules before you turn 65. Many people assume Medicare will cover excluded expenses because they were covered by a previous employer's health care plan. A good source of information is the *Medicare and You* handbook updated annually by the Centers for Medicare and Medicaid Services (CMS) and available at https://www.medicare.gov/medicare-and-you.

- **Manage Income Distributions**—Consult a financial advisor to explore strategies if your modified adjusted gross income (MAGI) is at or above the amount that triggers surcharges on Medicare Part B premiums. In 2020, MAGI over $87,000 for single filers and over $174,000 for married couples filing jointly will trigger additional income related monthly adjustment amount (IRMAA) premiums ranging from $202.40 to $491.60 versus the $144.60 standard premium.

- **Adjust Household Cash Flow**—Plan to spend more on health care in later life and factor it into your household budget. Compare Medicare Part B premiums to what you were paying previously for employer plan cost-sharing. Many people on Marketplace plans with premium tax credits experience "sticker shock" when they transition to Medicare/Medigap and insurance premium costs soar.

References

Benz, C. (2018). *There's No Magic Number for Self-Funding Long-Term Care*. Morningstar. https://www.morningstar.com/articles/887642/theres-no-magic-number-for-self-funding-long-term-care

Blanton, K. (2019). *Walk? Yes! But Not 10,000 Steps a Day*. Squared Away Blog. https://squaredawayblog.bc.edu/squared-away/walk-yes-but-not-10000-steps-a-day/

Changing from the Marketplace to Medicare (n.d.). HealthCare.gov. https://www.healthcare.gov/medicare/changing-from-marketplace-to-medicare/

Health Care Price Check: A Couple Retiring Today Needs $285,000 as Medical Expenses in Retirement Remain Relatively Steady (2019). Fidelity Investments: https://www.fidelity.com/bin-public/060_www_fidelity_com/documents/press-release/healthcare-price-check-040219.pdf

Hagen, K. (2019). *This 1 Expense Could Cost Retirees $285,000*. The Motley Fool. https://www.fool.com/retirement/2019/04/07/this-1-expense-could-cost-retirees-285000.aspx

Health Tips for Older Adults (n.d.). National Institute of Diabetes and Digestive and Kidney Diseases Health Information Center. https://www.niddk.nih.gov/health-information/weight-management/healthy-eating-physical-activity-for-life/health-tips-for-older-adults

Here's How Much Your Healthcare Costs Will Rise as You Age (2020). RegisteredNursing.Org. https://www.registerednursing.org/healthcare-costs-by-age/

Hernandez-Murillo, R. & Martinek, C.J. (2010). *In Some Cases, a Sick Economy Can Be a Prescription for Good Health*. Federal Reserve Bank of St. Louis. https://www.stlouisfed.org/publications/regional-economist/october-2010/in-some-cases-a-sick-economy-can-be-a-prescription-for-good-health

How to Plan for Rising Health Care Costs (2019). Fidelity Investments: https://www.fidelity.com/viewpoints/personal-finance/plan-for-rising-health-care-costs

Hulbert, M. (2019). *Is Early Retirement Hazardous to Your Health?* Marketwatch. https://www.marketwatch.com/story/is-early-retirement-hazardous-to-your-health-2019-11-25

9 Ways to Reduce Health Care Costs in Retirement (2018). *U.S. News and World Report.* https://money.usnews.com/money/retirement/medicare/articles/2018-03-21/9-ways-to-reduce-health-care-costs-in-retirement

O'Brien, S. (2020). *Here's How Much More You'll Pay for Medicare Part B in 2020.* CNBC. https://www.cnbc.com/2019/11/11/heres-how-much-more-youll-pay-for-medicare-part-b-in-2020.html

Sergent, J. (2019). Retirees Will Spend About $285,000 on Health Care, Fidelity Says. *Financial Advisor.* https://www.fa-mag.com/news/health-care-tab-for-retiring-couple-is-expected-to-hit--285-000-44158.html

Skerrett, P.J. (2015). *Is Retirement Good for Health or Bad for It?* Harvard Health Publishing. https://www.health.harvard.edu/blog/is-retirement-good-for-health-or-bad-for-it-201212105625

Stein, S. (2017). *Long-Term Care Insurance vs. Self-Insuring: What is Best for You?* Association for Long Term Care Planning. http://www.altcp.org/long-term-care-insurance-vs-self-insuring/

Sun, W., Webb, A., & Zhivan, N. (2010). *Does Staying Healthy Reduce Your Lifetime Health Care Costs?* Center for Retirement Research at Boston College. https://crr.bc.edu/briefs/does-staying-healthy-reduce-your-lifetime-health-care-costs/

The Impact of Retirement on Your Health (2017). South Shore Elder Services. https://sselder.org/wp-content/uploads/2013/03/QA-June-2017-Is-Retirement-Bad-For-Your-Health.pdf

What is the Difference Between Medicare Supplement Insurance Plans F, G, and N? (2020). eHealthMedicare. https://www.ehealthmedicare.com/faq/differences-between-medicare-supplement-plans-f-g-n/

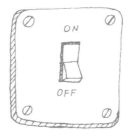

Chapter 10: Transitioning to Medicare

While about 9 in 10 older adults flip the Social Security "switch," the transition from employer, Affordable Care Act (ACA), or private health insurance to Medicare affects everyone. Medicare is a federal government health insurance program that covers some 59.8 million people age 65 and over and those under 65 with specific disabilities or permanent kidney failure (end-stage renal disease). It does not pay for all medical expenses but rather provides a fixed amount of coverage (adjusted annually for inflation) that can be supplemented with other plans, called Medigap policies, designed to wrap around it. For some people, the transition to Medicare can result in a large increase in health care expenses when subsidies provided by a former employer plan or an ACA Marketplace policy go away. Serious comparison-shopping is also required to select a Medigap policy.

The Social Security Administration (SSA) recommends applying for Medicare benefits three months before you turn 65, whether you are retired or not. Unlike Social Security, for which the full-retirement age is gradually increasing to age 67, full Medicare benefits are available at age 65. Those who are already receiving Social Security are automatically enrolled in Medicare and receive a Medicare card and a "Welcome to Medicare" packet about three months before their 65th birthday. Those who by age 65 are still working and/or are postponing Social Security benefits need to proactively contact the SSA to enroll in Medicare. The Medicare open-enrollment period takes place toward the end of each calendar year and provides an opportunity to make changes to your coverage, add or drop a Medicare Advantage or prescription drug plan, or return to Original Medicare.

There are four parts to Medicare:

- **Part A: Hospitalization Insurance**—Covers hospital services, such as bed and board, nursing services, drugs and injections (while hospitalized), blood, equipment and medical supplies, inpatient physical therapy, skilled nursing care, and hospice services. Eligibility conditions and annually adjusted deductibles and co-payments apply. Part A coverage is premium-free for most Medicare beneficiaries because it is paid for by payroll taxes collected from employers and people who are currently working.

- **Part B: Medical Insurance**—Covers physician services, outpatient health care, emergency care, and laboratory services. Again, there are eligibility conditions and annually adjusted deductibles and co-payments. Beneficiaries are charged a monthly premium for Medicare Part B coverage, which is deducted from their Social Security check or billed quarterly. In 2020, the standard monthly premium for Part B is $144.60 and the Part B deductible is $198. Income-Related Monthly Adjustment Amounts (IRMAAs) apply for high-income beneficiaries. People who work past age 65 and have adequate employer health benefits may decide to postpone enrollment in Part B since their medical coverage is already provided.

- **Part C: Medicare Advantage Plan**—Provides both drug and medical coverage, typically in a managed care plan format (e.g., HMOs and PPOs). Monthly Part C premiums vary by plan. Enrollment in Part C plans has grown steadily over the past two decades; about 22 million people had Medicare Advantage plans in 2019. The average Medicare Advantage plan premium for 2020 is $23 per month according to the U.S. Centers for Medicare & Medicaid Services (CMS). Plan participants pay their Part B premium and the premium for their Medicare Advantage plan, and a private insurer bundles their coverage into one plan.

- **Part D: Medicare Prescription Drug Plan**—Provides voluntary outpatient coverage for prescription drugs since it was created under the Medicare Modernization Act of 2003. Different Part D plans have varying costs and cover different drugs. Part D coverage is offered by hundreds of private insurance plans nationwide that meet standards established by Medicare. Beneficiaries pay a monthly premium, a yearly deductible, and part of the cost of their prescriptions (e.g., co-payments). Options to obtain Part D coverage include stand-alone prescription drug plans that provide drug coverage only and Medicare Advantage plans that provide both drug coverage and medical coverage. CMS recommends a 3-step process for selecting a Part D plan: determine which plans cover your drugs, the costs of each plan, and each plan's pharmacy and mail order options.

- **Get Educated on Medicare**—Review the annually updated CMS publication *Medicare and You*, available in print and online. There you will find information about signing up for Medicare, the parts of Medicare, Original Medicare (Parts A and B) versus Medicare Advantage plans, and Medigap policies. In addition to learning about Medicare, contact your employer's Human resources office to learn about available retiree health insurance benefits, if any, and how they dovetail with Medicare.

- **Get Help If Needed**—Learn more about Medicare and Medigap policies by contacting your local branch of the State Health Insurance Assistance Program (SHIP), where trained counselors provide information and assistance at no charge. The number for local SHIP offices (called SHINE in some states) can be obtained from county offices of senior services (a.k.a., area agencies on aging), from 800-633-4227 (the CMS Medicare Help Line), or from the website https://www.shiptacenter.org/.

- **Shop Around for Doctors**—Ask if doctors accept Medicare. According to CMS and the Kaiser Family Foundation, about 93 percent of doctors do. This means that they agree to Medicare's fee schedule as full payment for bills. The technical term for this is "Medicare assignment." Doctors who "accept assignment" agree to Medicare's payment terms. Similar to health insurance plans before age 65, if a doctor does not participate in Medicare, patients must shop around to find a new doctor that accepts assignment or pay the doctor out-of-pocket without any insurance coverage.

- **Keep Good Records**—Create a spreadsheet to keep track of health care expenses and insurance reimbursement. List expenses as rows in the spreadsheet and three possible payment sources—Medicare, a Medigap or former employer health insurance policy, and out-of-pocket funds—as columns. After decades of having only one health insurance company to deal with, having several payment sources in later life can get confusing and a spreadsheet will help create order.

- **Live a Healthy Lifestyle**—Try to avoid costly wealth-draining medical expenses by doing things that health and nutrition experts recommend. This includes eating healthy meals, participating in physical activity, not smoking, moderating alcohol consumption, and getting adequate sleep. In addition to a reduced risk for heart disease and certain cancers, recent research also suggests that these activities have protective effects against dementia.

- **Pay Attention to Open Enrollment**—Re-evaluate Medicare and Medigap policy options annually and consider making changes if you are dissatisfied with your current health plan or if you have experienced changes in health status. Each year, from October 15 through December 7, Medicare beneficiaries can switch from Original Medicare to a Medicare Advantage plan or vice versa. They can also pick up or drop a Part D prescription drug plan or switch from one Part D drug plan to another.

References

Boccuti, C., Fields, C., & Hamel, L. (2015). *Primary Care Physicians Accepting Medicare: A Snapshot.* Kaiser Family Foundation. https://www.kff.org/medicare/issue-brief/primary-care-physicians-accepting-medicare-a-snapshot/

Comparing Medicare Prescription Drug Coverage (2005). U.S. Centers for Medicare & Medicaid Services. https://njaes.rutgers.edu/health-finance/pdfs/medicare-drug-comparison-worksheet.pdf

Getting Started With Medicare (n.d.). U.S. Centers for Medicare & Medicaid Services. https://www.medicare.gov/sign-up-change-plans/get-started-with-medicare

Long-Term Study Investigates Association Between Self-Reported Diet in Midlife and Dementia Risk (2019). National Institute on Aging. https://www.nia.nih.gov/news/long-term-study-investigates-association-between-self-reported-diet-midlife-and-dementia-risk

Medicare and You 2020 (2019). U.S. Centers for Medicare & Medicaid Services. https://www.medicare.gov/sites/default/files/2019-09/10050-medicare-and-you.pdf

Medicare Costs at a Glance (2019). U.S. Centers for Medicare & Medicaid Services. https://www.medicare.gov/your-medicare-costs/medicare-costs-at-a-glance

Medicare Open Enrollment (2019). Medicareresources.org. https://www.medicareresources.org/glossary/medicare-open-enrollment/

Norris, L. (2019). *How are Medicare Benefits Changing for 2020?* Medicareresources.org. https://www.medicareresources.org/faqs/what-kind-of-medicare-benefit-changes-can-i-expect-this-year/

Total Number of Medicare Beneficiaries (2019). Kaiser Family Foundation. www.kff.org/medicare/state-indicator/total-medicare-beneficiaries/

2020 Medicare Parts A & B Premiums and Deductibles (2019). U.S. Centers for Medicare & Medicaid Services. https://www.cms.gov/newsroom/fact-sheets/2020-medicare-parts-b-premiums-and-deductibles

What Happens if My Medicare Doctor No Longer Accepts Medicare Payment? (2019). eHealth Medicare. https://www.ehealthmedicare.com/faq/doctor-no-longer-accepts-medicare/

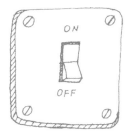

Chapter 11: Setting New Financial Goals

Financial goals are generally grouped into three time-related categories: short-term (less than three years away), medium-term (three to ten years away), and long-term (more than 10 years away). A frequently cited long-term goal is saving enough money to exit the labor force and live comfortably on accumulated savings and earned benefits (i.e., to retire). This is a "To Retirement" goal because it involves saving to reach a planned workforce exit date.

The next phase of financial goal-setting is "flipping a switch" to "Through Retirement" goals: things you want to experience or purchase during the remainder of your life. A more colloquial phrase is "Bucket List," a term derived from the 2007 film starring Morgan Freeman and Jack Nicholson. The film describes two terminally ill men who go on an extended road trip to complete a series of "wish list" activities before they "kick the bucket."

Studies by the Consumer Federation of America have shown that, at every income level, people who set goals and are "planners" save more, are more successful financially, and feel better about their finances, than those who do not plan ahead. Setting financial goals is similar to planning an airplane trip. In order to purchase a ticket, you need to determine where you are starting out (Point A), where you want to go (Point B), how much the "ticket" (financial goal) costs, and the time frame (deadline) for the itinerary.

A dream, such as "I want to be comfortable in later life," is too vague to create an action plan. A financial goal is specific with a date and estimated cost. For example, "I want to save $10,000 for a riverboat cruise in four years." Travel and entertainment, family and charitable gifting, car purchases, and home improvements are common financial goals in later life. Other issues of concern to older adults are emergency savings, income taxes, health care, long-term care, and estate and end-of-life planning.

Just like "To" goals that are achieved during working years, "Through" goals should be "SMART," an acronym for **S**pecific, **M**easurable, **A**ttainable, **R**ealistic, and **T**ime-Related. To get started, make a list of dreams on a "Bucket List" (see Figure 1). Then flesh each dream out by answering five key questions: who, what, when, where, and why. Include completion dates and dollar amounts for each goal and state exactly what you will do to achieve them. For example, "I will save $2,500 annually for the next four years to take my $10,000 riverboat cruise."

Keep re-writing your "Through" financial goals until they are specific and measurable. The more specific a goal, the easier it is to determine the required savings. Then, work backwards using Table 1 to break a large goal down into smaller monthly savings amount goals. Once you've "done the math," tell others about your goals, so they can hold you accountable. Track your progress periodically and make changes as needed.

Another option is to skip the extended savings process completely and simply withdraw money from savings, if you are an "ant" with ample assets. In this circumstance, you don't need to break a goal down into monthly savings deposits because you already have the money! Taking money out of savings will likely feel foreign for reasons described in Chapter 1. A withdrawal may feel like a "loss" because your account balance will decrease, but it's okay—this is why you saved the money. Keep reminding yourself that if you don't spend your money, someone else will!

Figure 1: My Financial Bucket List

Table 1: Financial Goal-Setting Worksheet

1 Goals	2 Approximate Amount Needed	3 Month & Year Needed	4 Number of Months to Save	5 Date to Start Saving	6 Monthly Amount to Save (2-4)
Short-Term (under 3 years)					
Medium Term (3-10 years)					
Long-Term (10 or more years)					

Financial goals provide a framework for investment decisions and help tailor your choices. For example, if you have a short-term goal, like a new car purchase in three years, you will want to keep this money liquid, so there is no loss of principal. Equity investments like stock or growth mutual funds would be a poor choice due to the historical volatility of the stock market in short time frames. On the other hand, if you have a long-term goal, like college savings for a newborn grandchild, cash assets are a poor choice due to the risk of loss of purchasing power from inflation.

The bottom line is that you should determine your financial goals before you invest and know what you're investing for. You can't reach a financial goal if you don't set one. As financial planners are fond of saying, "people don't plan to fail; they fail to plan"… and set financial goals.

- **Keep Setting Financial Goals**—Set goals that are personally meaningful and realistically achievable. While you may have already reached your biggest financial goal ever (saving money for financial security in later life), there are still goals ahead. Take cars, for example. If you are in your early 60s, you could be driving through your late 80s. It is rare that cars last 20 or 25 years, so you will probably buy two or three more cars during your remaining lifetime. According to Kelley Blue Book, the average cost for a new light vehicle in the United States in December 2019 was $38,948.

- **Spend, Don't Save**—Use existing savings for "Through" goals, consistent with the "paycheck" creation and required minimum distribution (RMD) guidelines discussed in Chapters 3 and 4. If you already have money set aside to take a trip or make a gift or buy a car, why put yourself through the long, drawn out process of saving for these goals? You've got this! After decades of frugal living and conscientious saving, it is time to enjoy the money you have saved and use it to fund your goals. If not now, when? Often, "later" becomes "never."

- **Go First Class**—Consider prudent spending upgrades if you can afford it. As noted above, "flipping a switch" to withdraw money from savings may feel strange and psychologically uncomfortable. Unfamiliar spending patterns can add to this discomfort when you have led a frugal lifestyle for four or five decades. Do it anyway, if you have the resources, for increased comfort and lasting memories. Examples include buying orchestra seats instead of those in the mezzanine for plays, suites instead of standard hotel rooms, and first (or, at least, business) class on airplane trips.

- **Develop Spending Action Plans**—Make a list of spending goals and actions you can take to achieve them. You will be doing exactly what you did as a saver for decades, only in reverse. Conscientious people often report feeling a sense of accomplishment when they cross action items off of a list. Spending lists maintain that positive psychological state. Consider the case of RMDs from tax-deferred savings plans. Develop goals for the money that remains after taxes. As noted in Chapter 4, this money can be spent, gifted, and/or resaved in taxable accounts. Ditto for discretionary income left over from pension benefits, Social Security, and other income sources.

- **Automate Spending and Gifting**—Set it and forget it. If withdrawing money from savings feels like a "loss," set it up to do so automatically to avoid experiencing that "pain" on a continual basis. Consider automating monthly income withdrawals using techniques, such as automatic withdrawals from mutual funds, interest payments from bonds and certificates of deposit (CDs), and qualified charitable distributions from traditional IRAs.

References

A Financial Professional's Guide to Working with Older Clients (n.d.). AARP and Financial Planning Association. https://www.aarp.org/content/dam/aarp/money/how_to_guides/2011-08/Financial%20Professional%20Guide%20Working%20Older.pdf

Achieving Better Finances: What Every Senior and Elderly American Should Think About (2019). Great Senior Living. https://www.greatseniorliving.com/articles/senior-finances

Average New-Vehicle Prices Up Nearly 2% Year-Over-Year in December 2019, According to Kelley Blue Book (2020). Kelley Blue Book. https://mediaroom.kbb.com/2020-01-03-Average-New-Vehicle-Prices-Up-Nearly-2-Year-Over-Year-in-December-2019-According-to-Kelley-Blue-Book

Fontinelle, A. (2019). *Setting Financial Goals for Your Future*. Investopedia. https://www.investopedia.com/articles/personal-finance/100516/setting-financial-goals/

Less Than Half of U.S. Households Report Good Savings Progress, According to 2016 America Saves Week Survey (2016). Consumer Federation of America. https://consumerfed.org/press_release/less-than-half-of-u-s-households-report-good-savings-progress-according-to-annual-america-saves-week-survey/

Set a Time Frame for Your Financial Goals (2019). FINRA. https://www.finra.org/investors/insights/set-time-frame-your-financial-goals

The Bucket List (2019). Wikipedia. https://en.wikipedia.org/wiki/The_Bucket_List.

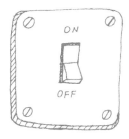

Chapter 12: You Can't Take It with You: Philanthropy and Estate Planning

As people get older, the phrase "You can't take it with you" takes on a new poignancy. This is especially true for ultra-saver "ants" when a financial advisor projects they will likely never run out of money during their lifetime. There are two solutions to this "problem," which, admittedly, comes from a place of privilege. You can either spend more money on "stuff" and/or experiences or gift it during your lifetime and/or following your death. To do the latter properly requires income tax savvy and estate planning documents.

About nine of 10 taxpayers took the standard deduction on their 2018 tax return, following passage of the Tax Cuts and Jobs Act (TCJA). The TCJA almost doubled previous standard deduction amounts, making standard deductions more cost-effective (i.e., tax-saving)—not to mention simpler—than itemizing. No need to save and tally up receipts! Standard deductions ($12,400 for single tax filers and $24,800 for couples filing jointly in 2020) are now a "high hurdle," especially for couples. As a result, many small donors who can't itemize no longer receive a tax write-off for charitable gifts, resulting in decreased charitable giving by individual Americans.

There are still ways that donors can benefit tax wise from charitable gifts. If you want to be more philanthropic in later life, consider these ideas:

- **"Bunch" Contributions**—Plan combined itemized deductions—including charitable donations—so they periodically exceed the standard deduction amount (e.g., every three to five years). "Bunch" them up into target years (e.g., years you expect to receive a higher-than-normal income). For example, $30,000 in gifts, along with $20,000 of other itemized deductions (e.g., mortgage interest and state and local taxes), is $25,200 greater than the standard deduction for couples ($50,000–$24,800), thereby saving thousands of dollars in taxes. If you itemize deductions, gifts of cash are deductible up to 60 percent of adjusted gross income (AGI). In 2020, as part of the Coronavirus Aid, Relief, and Economic Security (CARES) Act, that limit was suspended. In addition, taxpayers who do not itemize can take a deduction of up to $300 for qualified charitable contributions beginning in 2020.

- **Make Qualified Charitable Distributions**—Ask the custodian of your traditional individual retirement account (IRA) to make a direct transfer to a qualified charity. To do this, the account owner must be age 70 ½ or older. QCDs count toward satisfying required minimum distributions (RMDs) for the year (see Chapter 4). IRA owners can contribute up to $100,000 per year to charities with funds from their IRA without paying tax on the donated money. Otherwise, RMD withdrawals are taxed as ordinary income.

- **Gift Highly Appreciated Stock**—Avoid taxes upon the sale of stock shares by gifting shares directly to a charity. Shares must have been owned for at least one year. Donors avoid capital gains tax on the increased value of their stock shares and get a deduction (if they can itemize) of the fair market value of the stock on the day that it is donated. Charities win, also, because they get a larger donation versus what they would receive if a donor sold the stock and donated after-tax proceeds.

- **Use a Donor Advised Fund (DAF)**—Create a DAF, which is an investment account established solely to support IRS-qualified charitable organizations. DAFs can be funded with securities or cash via investment companies, like Vanguard, Schwab, and Fidelity. Donors take an immediate tax deduction for the full amount of their irrevocable DAF deposit, and gifts to charities are made whenever a donor wants. DAFs are often used in conjunction with the "bunching" strategy described above.

- **Make Gifts That Pay Income**—Consider charitable remainder trusts. Donors get a partial tax deduction (based on trust terms) for their gift and receive income from the gifted asset for the remainder of their life. After death (or a certain period), the remainder of donated assets goes to the designated charity. Charitable gift annuities are similar in concept and provide a partial tax deduction and lifetime income.

An estate plan is a plan for managing and distributing assets during someone's lifetime and/or following death. Gifting can be done via estate planning tools—specifically annual gift exclusions, wills, and trusts:

- **Annual Gift Tax Exclusion**—For 2020, the annual gift tax exclusion is $15,000 per gift recipient. Some people prefer to see others enjoy their gifts and gradually decrease their taxable estate value. For gifts above $15,000 donors can use their $11.58 million (in 2020) federal estate and gift tax exemption, which effectively shields most Americans' estates from federal taxation.

- **Wills**—A will is a legal document that appoints executors to perform tasks (e.g., inventorying assets, paying debts, and distributing bequests) necessary to carry out a deceased person's wishes. A formal will prepared by an attorney with two witnesses is best (less likely to be challenged than handwritten wills or wills created with online forms). In a will, donors name individuals and charitable organizations to receive their assets in either flat dollar amounts or percentages of estate value.

- **Trusts**—A trust is a legal document in which the creator (a.k.a., grantor) transfers assets to a third-party trustee (e.g., attorney or commercial bank trust department) to manage on behalf of the grantor and/or one or more beneficiaries. Trusts can be revocable or irrevocable. Their advantages include avoiding the probate process and increased control over the distribution of assets.

Philanthropy is as much a lifestyle transition as a financial one. People who have been "lukewarm" donors during their working years often step it up when they are older after realizing that they have more than enough money to meet their own needs. Beyond income and estate tax-saving opportunities, there are also emotional and physical health benefits. Like volunteers, donors are happier, live longer, and have lower blood pressure and stress levels according to multiple research studies. The act of giving activates parts of the brain associated with pleasure, promotes social connection, and evokes gratitude by both donors and recipients.

- **Be Deliberate, Not Impulsive**—Select charities whose work you admire. Examples include organizations that have outstanding humanitarian work publicized in local or national media or support a cause that you are passionate about and organizations that you are involved with as a volunteer or have helped you or your family or friends personally.

- **Check Potential Charities**—Investigate a charity's "administrative expense ratio," which describes how it allocates its budget between funding its mission (e.g., helping homeless people) and funding administrative costs and overhead. Compare the expense ratio of two or three charities with similar missions. Two good online resources are www.charitynavigator.org and www.guidestar.org.

- **Specify a Purpose**—Ask a potential gift recipient to set guidelines on your gift to conform to a desired purpose (e.g., scholarships for low-income students) that is aligned with the mission of the organization. Further, it is okay to follow up and ask what a past gift specifically accomplished. Most charities also produce an annual report that provides information on program results and use of donations.

- **Plan Your Donations**—Decide in advance to whom and how much to give by creating an annual charitable gifting budget that is aligned with the gifting strategies described above. Use the following worksheet to develop a plan. The amount you give to charities is a personal decision; make the amount meaningful to you. You can also decide to say no. Simply turn down requests for charities that are not in your budget or on your high-priority list.

Total Annual Charitable $_____
Gifting Budget

"A" List Charities

_____ $_____
_____ $_____
_____ $_____
_____ $_____
_____ $_____
_____ $_____
_____ $_____
_____ $_____

Miscellaneous unplanned charitable
contributions

"B" List Charities

_____ $_____
_____ $_____
_____ $_____
_____ $_____
_____ $_____
_____ $_____
_____ $_____
_____ $_____

"C" List Charities

_____ $_____
_____ $_____
_____ $_____
_____ $_____
_____ $_____
_____ $_____
_____ $_____
_____ $_____

References

Bea, S. (2016). *Wanna Give? This is Your Brain on a 'Helper's High.'* Cleveland Clinic. https://health.clevelandclinic.org/why-giving-is-good-for-your-health/

Brenner, S. (2019). *Ten QCD Rules for 2019 You Need to Know.* Ed Slott and Company, LLC. https://www.irahelp.com/slottreport/ten-qcd-rules-2019-you-need-know

Charitable Contributions (2019). IRS. https://www.irs.gov/publications/p526.

Crary, D. (2019). *Charitable Giving by Individual Americans Drops in 2018.* Associated Press. https://apnews.com/588db760548c4c0fb21861b988dca841

How a Donor-Advised Fund Works (2020). Schwab Charitable. https://www.schwabcharitable.org/public/charitable/donor_advised_funds

How Did the TCJA Affect Incentives for Charitable Giving? (2018). Tax Policy Center. https://www.taxpolicycenter.org/briefing-book/how-did-tcja-affect-incentives-charitable-giving

IRS Provides Tax Inflation Adjustments for Tax Year 2020 (2019). Internal Revenue Service. https://www.irs.gov/newsroom/irs-provides-tax-inflation-adjustments-for-tax-year-2020

James, R. (2018). *A Donor's Guide to the 2018 Tax Law.* Linked In. https://www.linkedin.com/pulse/donors-guide-2018-tax-law-russell-james-j-d-ph-d-cfp-

Kagan, J. (2020). Charitable Remainder Trust. *Investopedia.* https://www.investopedia.com/terms/c/charitableremaindertrust.asp

Kagan, J. (2018). Charitable Gift Annuity. *Investopedia.* https://www. investopedia.com/terms/c/charitable-gift-annuity.asp

Lankford, K. (2015). 5 Things You Should Know About Giving Stock to Charity. *Kiplinger's Personal Finance.* https://www.kiplinger.com/article/ taxes/T054-C001-S001-giving-stock-to-charity.html

Marsh, J. & Suttie, J. (2010). 5 Ways Giving is Good for You. *Greater Good Magazine.* https://greatergood.berkeley.edu/article/item/5_ways_giving_is_ good_for_you

Maximizing Tax Benefits by Concentrating or "Bunching" Charitable Contributions (2019). Schwab Charitable. https://www.schwabcharitable. org/public/file/P-11935800

Moskowitz, D. (2019). Estate Planning: Living Trusts vs. Simple Wills. *Investopedia.* https://www.investopedia.com/articles/personal-finance/070715/estate-planning-living-trusts-vs-simple-wills.asp

Reeves, J. (2017). *The Ultimate Guide to Estate Planning.* AARP. https:// www.aarp.org/money/budgeting-saving/info-2016/the-ultimate-guide-to-estate-planning.html

Tompor, S. & Menton, J. (2020). Taxes 2020: When to File and What changes to Expect. *USA Today.* https://www.usatoday.com/ story/money/2020/01/27/taxes-2020-what-changes-expect-filing-returns/4558347002/

What is a Donor-Advised Fund? (2020). Fidelity Charitable. https://www. fidelitycharitable.org/guidance/philanthropy/what-is-a-donor-advised-fund. html?

Wills, Trusts, and Probate (2020). Nolo. https ://www.nolo.com/legal-encyclopedia/wills-trusts-estates

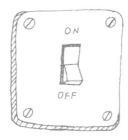

Chapter 13: Financial Organization and Simplification

Now is the time to get serious about streamlining your finances. Prior to leaving long-time careers, many people lead extremely busy lives. Between work, commuting, sleep, personal care, errands, and family responsibilities, there is little time left for all but the most basic financial management tasks, like paying household expenses and credit card bills. Once job constraints disappear, however, there are no more excuses! You now have time to flip this "switch" and take financial organization and simplification off the back burner. Remember, if you don't do this work, someone else (e.g., an adult child or attorney) will eventually have to, perhaps even to the detriment of your wishes.

You may have already experienced a wake-up call to simplify your financial life. Common triggers include dealing with a deceased parent's diminished capacity and/or unorganized finances, a move that required culling through boxes of old financial records, and the approach of age 72, the government-designated age for taking required minimum distribution (RMD) withdrawals from tax-deferred savings accounts (see Chapter 4). Another incentive to simplify is cost; unorganized finances can generate unnecessary expenses (e.g., bank fees and taxes).

Then there is the "Marie Kondo effect," named for the popular Netflix *Tidying Up With Marie Kondo* show hosted by Japanese organization consultant Marie Kondo. There was a notable upsurge in thrift shop donations after this show aired on January 1, 2019. Kondo's "KonMari" method of decluttering advises viewers to hold each of their possessions, ask themselves whether each item sparks joy, and thank items that don't spark joy for their past service before disposing of them. These principles of sorting, organizing, and simplifying can also be applied to personal finances and can make money easier to manage in later life.

You have probably taken some steps already to simplify your finances. For example, sources of regularly recurring income (e.g., paychecks, Social Security, and pension benefits) are automatically deposited into a checking or savings account. Direct deposit is safer and more convenient than having a paper check mailed to you and provides access to your money sooner. You may have also automated car loan payments, insurance premiums, and utility bills to save time and postage costs. The money needed to pay these bills is automatically withdrawn from a checking account or charged to a credit card (a side benefit of this is additional rewards points).

You may have also consolidated similar types of financial accounts. For example, when traditional IRAs became widely available in the early 1980s, some banks offered small appliances as an incentive to open accounts. You could have furnished an entire kitchen with blenders, toasters, and other appliances offered by different banks! Now, 40 or so years later, you may still have multiple IRAs. Consolidating accounts can lower account management fees, reduce account-related mail, and make it easier to determine RMD amounts.

Organizing and simplifying financial documents is not the most exciting way to spend a day, but the rewards are worth it. With organized records, you can find documents easily, handle tax disputes with confidence, document ownership of assets, potentially save money on tax bills (e.g., capital gains taxes), and help others handle your financial affairs, if necessary. You can also eliminate the stress associated with feeling disorganized. Having recently completed a major "possession purge" in advance of a 1,000+ mile interstate move, I can attest to the satisfaction and (yes, Marie Kondo) joy experienced when personal possessions and financial records are sorted, prioritized, and organized and only essential or bliss-inducing items are retained.

- **Create a Financial Inventory**—List key financial data in one document, including bank and brokerage accounts, insurance policies, credit card numbers, loans, names of financial advisors, and the location of key documents. A good template financial inventory form was developed by the Vanguard investment company and can be found at https://personal.vanguard.com/pdf/FM_inventory.pdf.

- **Continue to Consolidate Financial Assets**—Prepare a net worth statement (assets minus debts) and list all your financial accounts and their current balances. Many people have multiple brokerage and bank accounts, IRAs, and mutual funds. Identify like category assets that could be combined and consolidate similar assets with a minimum number of custodians (e.g., one traditional IRA instead of three).

- **Close Subpar Accounts**—Eliminate and replace accounts that charge high fees or do not offer competitive interest rates as part of your account consolidation process. Another good candidate for closure is mutual funds with high expense ratios, often because they include pesky 12(b)(1) fees that are assessed for marketing expenses.

- **Review and Update Beneficiary Designations**—Identify financial assets that have a beneficiary designation, including life insurance policies, IRAs, and tax-deferred employer retirement savings plans, and list them all in one place. Review your beneficiary designations and revise them as needed. Also designate contingent beneficiaries in case your first beneficiary designee predeceases you or is unable to serve.

- **Cull Automated Payments**—Review recurring bill payments that are automatically deducted from financial accounts and cancel those for discretionary products and services that are no longer used. Common examples include gym memberships, newspapers, "[X] of the month" clubs, and satellite radio fees, especially if you no longer commute a long distance and listen to a radio very much anymore

- **Purge and Shred**—Save year-end financial account statements, such as those for mutual funds, and shred the monthly or quarterly statements that came before. Save paper bank and credit card statements for up to a year or electronically using a computer flash drive. Retain tax records for up to seven years in the event of an audit and records for capital assets (e.g., stock) for as long as you hold them plus seven years.

- **Document Your Digital Assets**—Make a list of usernames, passwords, PINs, and other details related to your digital life. A good template can be found at https://njaes.rutgers.edu/money/pdfs/Digital-Assets-Work-sheet.pdf. Examples of digital assets include benefit (e.g., airline frequent flyer and retailer loyalty program), e-mail, financial, online merchant, organization, and social media accounts. Make sure that several trusted individuals can access your digital inventory information, if needed, but keep this information in a safe place otherwise.

- **Check Your Credit History**—Request a free credit report once every four months from one of the "Big Three" credit reporting agencies. For example, check Experian in April, Equifax in August, and TransUnion in December. Review written or online reports carefully for evidence of incorrect information or identity theft.

- **Prepare or Review Estate Planning Documents**—Review each of your estate planning documents (e.g., will, living will, and power of attorney) to make sure that they still reflect your wishes. Also make sure that all parties named in your documents (e.g., executor, guardian) are alive and still willing and able to serve. You should repeat this review every two to three years or sooner if life circumstances change (e.g., divorce and remarriage).

- **Organize a Home Financial Center**—Designate one place in your home to store your financial records and perform routine financial tasks, such as bill paying and reconciling your checking account balance. Your financial center can include a computer, desk, table, filing drawer, and/or cabinet. The choice is up to you.

References

Managing Your Money in Old Age (2019). *Kiplinger's Personal Finance.* https://www.kiplinger.com/article/retirement/T023-C000-S004-managing-your-money-in-old-age.html

Marie Kondo Isn't Sparking Joy for Thrift Stores (2019). *The Wall Street Journal* https://www.wsj.com/articles/marie-kondo-persuaded-you-to-jettison-your-junk-thrift-stores-sayenough-11551889124

9 Ways to Simplify Your Life (2019). Next Avenue https://www.nextavenue.org/9-ways-simplify-your-financial-life/

Organizing Your Finances (2015). University of Wisconsin Extension https://washington.extension.wisc.edu/files/2017/10/Issue-8-Organizing-UW-Ext.pdf

The Marie Kondo Effect: What to Do With All the Stuff That Doesn't 'Spark Joy.' ABC News https://abcnews.go.com/GMA/Living/marie-kondo-effect-stuff-spark-joy/story?id=60446673

The Tidying Tide: Marie Kondo Effect Hits Sock drawers and Consignment Stores (2019). *The Washington Post.* https://www.washingtonpost.com/lifestyle/home/the-tidying-tide-marie-kondo-effect-hits-sock-drawers-and-consignment-stores/2019/01/10/234e0b62-1378-11e9-803c-4ef28312c8b9_story.html

Your Personal Financial Inventory (2014). Vanguard. http://www.vanguard.com/pdf/FM_inventory.pdf

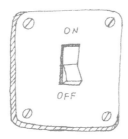

Chapter 14: Becoming Fraud Bait

Willie Sutton, the famous bank robber, was reportedly asked why he robbed banks and replied, "Because that's where the money is." For this same reason, older adults are frequent targets for fraud. Baby Boomers (age 56 to 74 in 2020) are currently the wealthiest generation in American history. According to the Federal Trade Commission (FTC), people age 60 and over are 20 percent less likely than younger adults to report losing money to fraud; however, when they *are* scam victims, their losses are higher. Median losses to fraud in 2018 were $600, $769, and $1,700, respectively, for ages 60 to 69, 70 to 79, and 80 and older.

Becoming "fraud bait" is not a "switch" that anyone seeks out, but the aging process flips it anyway. In addition to having assets and excellent credit, some older adults are isolated and have decreased cognitive function. Some fraudsters approach older adults as friendly and sympathetic "helpers" while others intimidate them through fear and misinformation. Lack of tech savvy is another key factor. An Aspen Institute study found that older adults had difficulty navigating online FBI fraud-reporting forms. The FTC found that people age 60 and over were about five times more likely than younger people to report losing money on tech scams because they are less savvy handling e-mails, surfing the internet with updated browsers and firewalls, and maintaining computer anti-virus software.

Fraud also happens because older adults expose themselves to more sales situations compared to the general population. An AARP study found that victims age 50+ were more likely to engage in "at risk" activities, including opening and reading junk mail, entering their names in drawings to win prizes, and attending "free meal" seminars with sales presentations, while also being less likely to sign up for the Do Not Call list and check references before hiring someone. A report on free meal seminars by the North American Securities Administrators Association (NASAA) noted, "A combination of 'free lunch' seminars, misleading 'senior specialist' designations, and abusive sales practices can create a perfect storm for investment fraud."

Below is a description of four common older adult scams that are frequently reported to the FTC:

- **Tech Support Scams**—Victims are scammed by a pop-up message purporting to come from companies like Apple, Microsoft, and Norton stating their computer is infected. The message says that they must immediately call a phone number or click on a link or risk losing personal data. If victims take the bait, fraudsters steal personal information or install malware to access sensitive data.

- **Imposter Scams**—Victims can be scammed under several false pretenses including imposters purporting to be government officials (e.g., IRS and Social Security) or relatives (e.g., a grandchild) in trouble. Fraudsters request that they wire money immediately to pay "taxes" or "fees" or to help someone out.

- **Lottery Scams**—Victims receive a letter with a fake check for a lottery, prize, or sweepstakes and are told that they must respond immediately to pay "taxes" or "customs duties" or some type of fee. Fraudsters ask for bank account information or a credit card number or ask victims to wire them money. The fake check bounces, of course, and victims lose money and even get requests for more money.

- **Romance Scams**—Victims are scammed by fraudsters who troll online dating sites. Scammers, who say they live far away due to a job or military service, build a relationship with victims online via email and phone calls and eventually request money for something urgent.

Fraudsters often request a wire transfer of funds and coach victims what to say to not arouse the suspicion of bank officials.

In addition, there are charity, funeral, investment, and contractor scams, and more. Regardless of the type of scam, red flags of fraud include requests to wire money immediately, requests for payment using gift cards or prepaid debit cards, requests for payment in advance of services, and secrecy ("Don't tell anyone").

- **Never Sign Blank Forms**—Draw a line through blank spaces or refuse to sign suspicious forms. You never know what information could be added later (e.g., high interest rates or fees). "Blank line" fraud can be found for insurance claims, "investments," contracting scams, and more. Also, do not buy anything that you could not explain simply to another person.

- **Walk Away From "Guaranteed" Investments**—Be suspicious of guaranteed higher-than-market-rate returns—think Bernie Madoff's failed Ponzi scheme that paid unusually consistent returns despite fluctuations in market performance. Apart from CDs, bonds, and other fixed-income securities, investment returns typically vary with market conditions. Take time to ask questions, check out unfamiliar companies and charities, and request references. If something sounds too good to be true, it probably is.

- **Use Caution with Free Meal Seminars**—Heed warnings from AARP and NASAA. Free meal seminars set people up for potentially unscrupulous and abusive sales practices. I recently attended one "undercover" and observed typical red flags: a speaker with no credentials like CFP®, loaded phrases like "eliminate market risk," and door-prize drawings to garner contact information. Personally, I left the address section blank and listed my disconnected phone number and a "junk" email address.

- **Ditch Your Landline**—Consider this option (if your cellular service is reliable) to reduce potentially fraudulent robocalls coming into your home. Yes, robocallers can still call your cell phone, but the volume of calls will be reduced and you can block future calls from each robocaller. In addition to reducing phone call volume, you will also save on landline charges and taxes.

- **Get on the Do Not Call List**—Register up to three cell and/or landline phone numbers at once at https://www.donotcall.gov/. It only takes a minute to type your phone number(s), verify the number(s), and click an email link to register your phone(s). Be aware, however, that the Do Not Call Registry is not perfect and excludes political groups, charities, surveys, and debt collectors. For this reason, also use caller ID and cell phone call blocking.

- **Recognize "Red Flag" Language**—Delete or hang up on any solicitation using phrases like "You must act now or the offer will go away," "You won [X], but you first have to pay a fee for [Y]," and "You must 'verify' your account number," or requests to pay "unpaid taxes" with a prepaid debit card. In addition, if callers sound robotic or fake, they likely are. Hang up and block them.

- **Do Not Pay in Advance for Services**—Be suspicious of requests for full payment in advance of services and do not agree to these terms. Instead, require contractors to bill for a series of gradual payments as work is performed to your satisfaction.

- **Power Down**—If a tech scam pops up on your computer, it will likely lock your browser. Do not click the link or call the suggested phone number. Rather, power down, wait a few minutes, and power up. The pop up should disappear. Install Malwarebytes and consult an IT professional if these problems persist. Another computer scam that also may require professional assistance is ransomware, where scammers encrypt a victim's files and demand a ransom to restore access.

References

Elderly Fraud Scams: How They're Being Targeted and How to Prevent It (2020). The Fraud Examiner. https://www.acfe.com/fraud-examiner. aspx?id=4294997223

Fair, L. (2019). *Scams and Older Consumers: Looking at The Data.* Federal Trade Commission. https://www.consumer.ftc.gov/blog/2019/10/scams-and-older-consumers-looking-data

Fazzini, K. (2019). *Here's How Online Scammers Prey on Older Americans and What They Should Know to Fight Back.* CNBC. https://www.cnbc.com/2019/11/23/new-research-pinpoints-how-elderly-people-are-targeted-in-online-scams.html

Fletcher, E. (2019). *Older Adults Hardest Hit by Tech Support Scams* (2019). FTC Consumer Protection Data Spotlight. https://www.ftc.gov/news-events/blogs/data-spotlight/2019/03/older-adults-hardest-hit-tech-support-scams

Imposter Scams (n.d.). Federal Trade Commission. https://www.consumer.ftc.gov/features/feature-0037-imposter-scams

James, B.D., Boyle, P.A., & Bennett, DA (2014). Correlates of Susceptibility to Scams in Older Adults Without Dementia. *Journal of Elder Abuse and Neglect*, 26(2), 107-122. https://www.ncbi.nlm.nih.gov/pubmed/24499279

O'Neill (2020). *Undercover "Barbservations" from a "Free Dinner" Seminar.* Money Talk. https://moneytalk1.blogspot.com/2020/01/undercover-barbservations-from-free.html

Pak, K. & Shadel, D. (2011). AARP Foundation National Fraud Victim Study. AARP. https://assets.aarp.org/rgcenter/econ/fraud-victims-11.pdf

Protecting Older Consumers 2018-2019. (2019). Federal Trade Commission. https://www.ftc.gov/system/files/documents/reports/protecting-older-consumers-2018-2019-report-federal-trade-commission/p144401_protecting_older_consumers_2019_1.pdf

Scams Targeting Older Adults (2019). MyCreditUnion.gov. https://www.mycreditunion.gov/fraud-prevention-center/scams/older-adults

Senior Investor Alert: Free Meal Seminars (2019). North American Securities Administrators Association (NASAA). https://www.nasaa.org/1950/senior-investor-alert-free-meal-seminars/

Skiba, K. (2019). *Americans Age 60+ Are Vulnerable to Tech-Support Scams, Government Warns.* AARP. https://www.aarp.org/money/scams-fraud/info-2019/ftc-older-consumers-report.html

Singletary, M. (2019). This Might Surprise You. Seniors Are Not More Susceptible to Scams; Younger Adults Are. *The Washington Post.* https://www.washingtonpost.com/business/2019/10/28/this-might-surprise-you-seniors-are-not-more-susceptible-scams-younger-adults-are/

Tech Support Scams (n.d.). Federal Trade Commission. https://www.ftc.gov/tips-advice/business-center/small-businesses/cybersecurity/tech-support-scams

Tedder, M. (2019). Not all Millennials are Broke. Over 600,000 are Now Millionaires. *Money.* https://money.com/rich-millennials-how-many-millionaires/

Top 10 Financial Scams Targeting Seniors (n.d). National Council on Aging. https://www.ncoa.org/economic-security/money-management/scams-security/top-10-scams-targeting-seniors/

What You Need to Know About Romance Scams (n.d.). Federal Trade Commission. https://www.consumer.ftc.gov/articles/what-you-need-know-about-romance-scams

Willie Sutton (n.d.). Federal Bureau of Investigation. https://www.fbi.gov/history/famous-cases/willie-sutton

"You've Won" Scams (n.d.). Federal Trade Commission. https://www.consumer.ftc.gov/features/pass-it-on/youve-won-scams

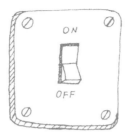

Chapter 15: Achieving Financial Peace of Mind

Like Chapters 1, 2, and 6, which discuss later life spending, parts of this final chapter of Part 1 come from a vantage point of privilege. Thus, it is important to acknowledge the financial realities of many older adults. The fact is, many people will struggle financially throughout their later years. According to the Center for Retirement Research (CRR) at Boston College, nearly a third of households nearing retirement have no retirement savings and the typical savings balance in 401(k)/IRA assets is about $135,000, which, if annuitized, would provide about $600 per month. The CRR provides this sobering assessment: "The future will see an increasing number of older retirees relying on small 401(k) balances and Social Security checks." Consequences of inadequate savings to support later life expenses include: working much longer than planned, "permadebt" (i.e., permanent debt), scrambling to get by, financial and emotional distress, relying on family members for housing and/or support, and major downward lifestyle adjustments (e.g., moving from a house to a tiny apartment).

New expenses begin, and many existing expenses increase in later life, adding pressure to constrained incomes. Some common "budget busters" include Medicare Part B premiums, health care expenses, new car purchases, major home repairs (e.g., roof replacement), dental care, home maintenance services (e.g., lawn care), taxes (e.g., pension, Social Security, and required minimum distributions), travel, "Bank of Mom and Dad" withdrawals by adult children, new retiree spending sprees, housing, and the financial impact of widowhood. In addition, inflation will eat into future purchasing power. According to the U.S. Bureau of Labor Statistics *CPI Inflation Calculator*, to have the same purchasing power of $50,000 in January 2000 would require $76,228 in October 2019—that's a 52 percent increase! Cost of living adjustments (COLAs) for inflation for most people are modest, however, such as the 1.6 percent increase in 2020 Social Security benefits.

The ultimate financial "flipped switch" is achieving "financial peace of mind." According to financial blogger Sharon O'Day, financial peace of mind can be defined as "knowing you will be okay for the rest of your life." She goes on to explain:

> It means you're not worried about having a roof over your head and food on the table in a place that feels safe and secure. It means your lifestyle is affordable. You have activities that can generate income if you need to supplement going forward. You have a financial cushion of some sort, big or small. You have rid yourself of major money-suckers like debt and spending habits that are not coherent with the life you want to lead…long term. The result of Financial Peace of Mind is feeling grounded.

With financial peace, the most basic needs of survival and security on the Maslow Hierarchy of Needs are covered, as well as some higher order human needs. "Ants" who have been conscientiously saving for decades may already have the resources for financial peace of mind (although they may not realize it), while "grasshoppers" who have been more focused on day-to-day finances than future goals will need to do some catch-up savings and/or major lifestyle adjustments. See Chapter 6 for specific strategies (e.g., working longer and geographic arbitrage).

When people realize that they have achieved financial peace of mind, they can change the way that they manage money and live their lives. Sometimes all it takes is a financial calculator or a Certified Financial Planner® (CFP®) or other trusted advisor to point out that you have reached the "finish line" and are in excellent financial health. Financial blogger Dennis

Friedman described his reactions when his financial advisor told him that he was not going to run out of money:

> Financial security buys peace of mind. It allows you to live a life without worrying about money. It gives you a sense of calmness. When I'm experiencing the finer things in life, I no longer worry about how much they're costing me. When I have dinner at a nice restaurant, I have a new sense of appreciation for the food and wine. My advice: Hire a fee-only financial advisor, so you feel more confident about your spending. It helped me and now I'm enjoying retirement far more.

Similarly, long-time *Wall Street Journal* columnist Jonathan Clements describes a five-step continuum for how people think about money ranging from those who are struggling to those who have achieved financial independence:

1. Head above water (starting to become more disciplined about personal finances);

2. Thinking about tomorrow (setting goals and saving);

3. Hitting the accelerator (saving larger dollar amounts);

4. Ahead of the game (higher wealth than peers and on the cusp of financial freedom); and

5. Hardly a second thought (spending as you wish without paying much heed to money).

Clements describes the financial peace achieved in Step 5 as follows:

> No doubt you could save $10 on the weekly grocery bill if you paid more attention. No doubt you eat out perhaps a little too often. No doubt your investment mix could be fine-tuned. But let's face it: It probably wouldn't make a

whole lot of difference and at this juncture, who needs the worry?

Saving can be a very "sticky" habit that is hard to break. However, if you have all the money you need, saving is probably no longer necessary. Do not die with substantial assets that you could have enjoyed. Use them to live your best life.

HOW TO FLIP THIS SWITCH

- **Do a Status Check**—Run a Monte Carlo analysis (see Chapter 2) or consult a CFP®, Human Resources counselor, or tax-deferred account custodian to determine if you have saved enough money to not have to worry about money. If you, indeed, have the resources required for financial peace of mind, stop, pivot, and start making plans to devote your time and money to doing things that you love.

- **Answer the Hard Question**—Ask yourself why you are slow to spend down savings that were intended for later life, especially after learning that you have more than enough money to last a lifetime. Is it fear of seeing account balances go down after decades of steady growth? Fear of future health care or long-term care expenses? Fear of pulling money out of stocks or stock funds on a day that the Dow drops 500 points? Not knowing how much or how little to withdraw? Once you analyze your fears, you can begin to address them and make changes in spending, time use, and more.

- **Make a Spending Projection**—Write down your current income and expenses (i.e., budget). Then make a revised spending plan with projections for income and expenses after full-time employment ends. Be sure to include any of the "budget busters" noted above and income withdrawals from investments, including required minimum distributions. Study the numbers carefully, so that you can feel comfortable knowing that you have enough money to insulate yourself from financial worries. If applicable, wean adult children off "subsidies," such as car insurance premium payments, free room and board, and a family cellphone plan.

- **Self-Insure for "The Big Unknown"**—Earmark a portion of savings for long-term care, so you can stop hoarding money for this expense. Start with an online search of the average cost of nursing homes in your home state. For example, it would cost $10,646 per month ($127,752 per year) in my former state of New Jersey and $8,152 per month ($97,824 per year) in my current state of Florida for a semi-private room. The average stay in a nursing home is 835 days (2.3 years), so multiply the annual cost by at least 2.3. Adjust upward (e.g., 3-4 years) to add a "cushion" for longer stays and/or additional expenses for in-home care or assisted living, especially if you will not have potential unpaid caregivers (e.g., adult children) to assist you.

References

Anspach, D. (2019). *How to Organize Your Finances for Retirement.* The Balance. https://www.thebalance.com/how-to-organize-your-finances-for-retirement-2388370

Breeding, B. (2016). *So I'll Probably Need Long-Term Care, But For How Long?* My LifeSite. https://www.mylifesite.net/blog/post/so-ill-probably-need-long-term-care-but-for-how-long/

Chatzky, J. (2019). *Biggest Retirement Budget Drainers and Ways to Lessen the Blow.* Financial Freedom Studio. https://www.jackson.com/financialfreedomstudio/articles/2019/05/biggest-retirement-budget-drainers-and-how-to-lessen-the-blow.html

Clements, J. (2019). *Out of the Swamp.* Humble Dollar. https://humbledollar.com/2019/02/out-of-the-swamp/

Cost of Living Adjustment (COLA) Information for 2020 (2019). Social Security Administration. https://www.ssa.gov/cola/

CPI Inflation Calculator (2019). U.S. Department of Labor Bureau of Labor Statistics. https://www.bls.gov/data/inflation_calculator.htm

Fried, M. (2019). Avoiding the New Retirement Spending Spree. *Kiplinger's Personal Finance.* https://www.kiplinger.com/article/retirement/T037-C032-S014-avoiding-the-new-retirement-spending-spree.html

Friedman, D. (2019). *Peace of Mind.* Humble Dollar. https://humbledollar.com/2019/11/peace-of-mind/

La Gorce (2019). Don't Save Too Little, or Too Much. *The New York Times.* https://www.nytimes.com/2019/11/06/your-money/retirement-savings.html

Maslow's Hierarchy of Needs (2018). Simply Psychology. https://www.simplypsychology.org/maslow.html

Nursing Home Costs (2019). Senior Living. https://www.seniorliving.org/nursing-homes/costs/

O'Day, S. (2013). *Financial Peace of Mind is Not What You Think It Is*. Senior Correspondent. http://www.seniorcorrespondent.com/articles/2013/09/30/financial-peace-of-mind-is-not-what-you-think-it-is.685776

Rose, J. (2017). 9 Financial Advisors Share What Happens When You Don't Save for Retirement. *Forbes*. https://www.forbes.com/sites/jrose/2017/01/27/9-financial-advisors-what-happens-when-you-dont-save-for-retirement/#4d00f1747ff3

Rosen, S. (2019). Kids and Money: It May Be Time to Ease Your Kid Off Bank of Mom and Dad. *The Chicago Tribune*. http://www.chicagotribune.com/business/success/sns-201908221506--tms--kidmoneyctnsr-a20190830-20190830-story.html

Rutledge, M. & Sanzenbacher, G.T. (2019). *What Financial Risks Do Retirees Face in Late Life?* Center for Retirement Research at Boston College. https://crr.bc.edu/wp-content/uploads/2018/12/IB_19-1.pdf

PART 2: Social Transitions

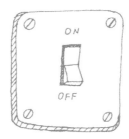

Chapter 16: Answering the "What Do You Do?" Question

It is only a matter of time. Eventually, after leaving a long-time career, someone—often a stranger—will ask the question: "What do you do for a living?" After decades of confidently and effortlessly stating "I am a [insert job title]" or "I work for [insert employer name]," how will you respond? With a simple "I'm retired," with "I used to [insert previous job description or employer]," or with a response that describes your current interests, passions, and pastimes? This chapter will help you develop a satisfactory answer.

First, it's important to determine how you feel about "R words" ("retirement," "retire," and related derivatives). If you want to avoid "R words," you will need to talk around them and craft another response. Many people, myself included, bend over backwards to avoid using words like "retired" or "retiree" in reference to ourselves for one reason or another. Below are some commonly cited reasons for avoiding "R words":

- They are often misinterpreted to mean that people focus exclusively on leisure and are no longer productive;

- Many older adults feel that they have valuable knowledge, skills, and the ability to contribute to society and "retired" seems dismissive;

- Strong identification with a career that took decades to build throughout adulthood can be hard to relinquish;

- The fastest growing segment of the American workforce is employees age 65 and older;

- Negative perceptions (e.g., uselessness, irrelevance, obsolescence, diminishment, and disengagement);

- Images of bored older adults in poor physical health endlessly watching television and other stereotypes that pervade the social conscience; and/or

- Societal messages and/or observations that directly or indirectly indicate that "your best days are behind you."

Not surprisingly, new "R words" were invented to alternatively describe the process of leaving a long-time job without the ageist stereotypes associated with "retirement" that suggest a withdrawal from an active life. Alternatives include "reinvention," "refirement," "rewirement," "reimagining," "rebooting," "re-engaging," and "retooling." The problem with these words is that they all begin with "re," a prefix that means "again," "repetition," or "going back." Author Shirley Showalter notes "a word beginning with 're' faces backward. The connotations associated with 're'—that 'real' life was in the past—are hard to shake, no matter how powerful the substitute for '-tire.'"

Others have taken to using non-"re" words in an attempt to avoid using an "R word" at all to describe themselves. Some examples include "Arrivement," Life 2.0, Encore Years, Next Act, Next Chapter (of life), and "Jubilee" or "Jubilation." The problem with these words, however, is that they are vague and/or not well understood, and require an additional explanation to fully describe what you do, which might often, then, lead to using "R words" anyway (e.g., "It's similar to retirement but…")

A third alternative to using "re" words and vague words is to describe yourself with language of your own choosing. To do this, first develop a plan to reinvent yourself by answering the question "How can I be useful in some capacity?" Visualize who you want to become. Next, make conscious decisions about your transition from a long-term career to "next steps." Share your plans with others for accountability, feedback, and support.

I have used this third strategy for almost two years in a deliberate effort to change the "R word" conversation about myself. When people said, "I hear you are retiring," or "Congratulations on your retirement!" I replied, "I am not retiring. I am simply leaving Rutgers University." I then described work I already had lined up (including this book) to make it clear that I fully intend to remain a player in the financial education field. Since I left Rutgers, I introduce myself this way: "I am the owner and CEO of a small business called Money Talk. I write, speak, and review content about personal finance." Bottom Line: it is my language and my "What do you do?" story. Similarly, everyone needs to create a "What do you do?" response that is right for them. There is no one "right" answer.

There are many ways to describe your life after work in addition to working at a new job or small business. Options include: volunteer work ("I am a cashier for the hospital thrift shop."), family responsibilities ("I take care of my four grandchildren."), hobbies ("I make pottery."), club affiliations ("I am president of the local Rotary Club."), and more. It is also okay to be intentionally vague if you want to ("I do whatever I want, when I want.") or even humorous ("I do as little as possible."). Answers to the "What do you do?" question will likely change over time as you get older.

- **Dodge the "R Words"**—Do not allow others to impose their "social clock" (i.e., expectations of what life events should occur at certain ages) upon you with comments like "You are 65. So when are you going to retire?" Instead, pivot and talk about what is next within your life or work if this situation makes you uncomfortable.

- **Practice Identity Bridging**—Maintain or enhance key aspects of your life that existed before you left full-time employment and will be continuing. This is especially important when you identify strongly with work. In my case, skills that I use for freelance work through Money Talk are the same skills that I used as a university professor.

- **Continue Regular Commitments**—Continue meaningful work projects on your own after you leave an employer. They will help build your new brand and provide a sense of meaning and structure. Examples include blogs, podcasts, webinars, videos, and social media.

- **Inventory Your Skill Set**—Make a list of your top work-related skills. Many will be transferrable to a new job, business, volunteer work, or hobby. Create a vision of who you want to be and take steps to put your dreams into action (e.g., networking and training or certification programs).

- **Avoid "Formerly" and "Used to Be"**—Focus your language on who you are *now* rather than what you did in the past. In addition to fostering future-mindedness, you become a more interesting person. As time goes on, people will be increasingly more interested in your current pursuits than what you used to do for a living.

- **Give It Time**—Give your "new self" and relationships time to evolve. Focus your efforts on sources of joy and meaning in your life. If a job was your identity, create a new work-based identity that provides daily time structure and social interaction. Do not try to fit a "mold" that will make you unhappy just because it's what you think "retired" people should do.

- **Develop an "Elevator Speech"**—Be prepared for the "What do you do?" question with a short one- or two-sentence reply. Keep in mind that your response could change over time as you move from the liberation (first post-work year) to the reorientation (2 to 15 years later) and reconciliation (more than 15 years later) phases of post-career life.

- **Find Mentors**—Ask people with several years of experience living in retirement to "show you the ropes" just like you found mentors at work to help you throughout your career. Ask them to describe steps that they took to live their current lifestyle and any lessons they learned along the way.

- **Get New Business Cards**—Introduce yourself to others with a post-career business card and decide what you want it to say. Business cards can include information about a job, a business, a new home address (e.g. as a calling card to meet your neighbors), or hobbies. A friend of mine who travels frequently has a business card that reflects her passions of "Wining, Dining, and Travel."

References

Allen, S. (2019). *When What You Do is No Longer Who You Are.* The University of Chicago Magazine. https://mag.uchicago.edu/law-policy-society/when-what-you-do-no-longer-who-you-are

Amabile, T. (2019). How Retirement Changes Your Identity. *Harvard Business Review.* https://hbr.org/ideacast/2019/01/how-retirement-changes-your-identity

Burton, J. (2019). *You're Probably Not Ready to Retire-Psychologically.* Marketwatch. https://www.marketwatch.com/story/why-youre-probably-not-psychologically-ready-to-retire-2019-05-21

Casey, J. (2019). *So, What Do You Do?* Retirement Wisdom. https://www.retirementwisdom.com/so-what-do-you-do/

Higgins-Dunn. (2019). *Older Workers are America's Fastest-Growing Labor Pool- And the Least Protected From Workplace Discrimination.* CNBC. https://www.cnbc.com/2019/04/13/older-workers-are-fastest-growing-labor-pool-and-the-least-protected.html

Hopkins, J. (2018). *Rewirement: Rewiring the Way You Think About Retirement.* Amazon Digital Services.

Lowry, B. (2012). *I'm Retired: So Who Am I Now?* Next Avenue. https://www.nextavenue.org/im-retired-so-who-am-i-now/

Re- (2019). Dictionary.com. https://www.dictionary.com/browse/re-

Showalter, S.H. (2017). A Better Way to Say "I'm Retired." *Forbes.* https://www.forbes.com/sites/nextavenue/2017/01/10/a-better-way-to-say-im-retired/#67b0386a7c7b

Sightings, T. (2019). 6 Things You Learn After Retirement. *U.S. News and World Report.* https://money.usnews.com/money/blogs/on-retirement/articles/6-things-you-learn-after-retirement

Skene, P. (2016). *A New Word for Retirement: "Arrivement."* SixtyandMe. https://sixtyandme.com/a-new-word-for-retirement-arrivement/

Smolowe, J. (2016). The Reason I Hate the Word 'Retirement.' *Forbes.* https://www.forbes.com/sites/nextavenue/2016/03/11/the-reason-i-hate-the-word-retirement/

Social Clock (2019). American Psychological Association. https://dictionary.apa.org/social-clock

The Five Stages of Retirement (2007). Age Wave. https://agewave.com/the-five-stages-of-retirement/

Weeks, L. (2013). *Maybe We Should Retire the Word 'Retire'.* NPR. https://www.npr.org/2013/03/28/175461789/maybe-we-should-retire-the-word-retire

What is Refirement? (2019). The Refirement Group. http://www.refirement.com/Pages/WhatIsReFirementPage.html

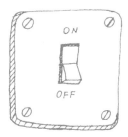

Chapter 17: Changed Relationships with Family and Friends

Two things happen when people step away from long-time employment—they have more unstructured time and they are no longer tethered to a specific geographic location by a job. In many ways, their future is like a blank slate. There are options to continue working (or not), move close to or away from family members (or not), and get more involved in new or existing hobbies and organizations (or not).

Having more free time and the ability to relocate (if finances permit) can also trigger changes in relationships with a spouse, family members, and friends. While working can make it difficult to provide daily care for an elderly parent or grandchildren, live closer to parents or adult children, and spend more time with friends, these time-intensive activities are possible, and often desirable, in post-career years.

There is a television commercial for Fidelity Investments in which an older couple tells their financial advisor that their daughter is having twins. First, the couple wants to set up a college savings account for the twins (change in plans #1), next, they want to move closer to their grandchildren (change in plans #2), and, lastly, the grandmother wants to explore a new career as an artist (change in plans #3).

Marriages can change considerably post-career. First, there is the timing of each spouse's workplace exit. Do they leave their respective jobs at the same time or separately? Then there is the simple fact that they are spending more time together than, perhaps, ever before. For many couples with two employed spouses, much of their time was spent apart working, commuting, and attending work-related events. When they are free from workplace demands and have 40 or more hours per week of newly freed up time, there are issues related to "how much time together is too much?," personal space, and separate versus common interests. Differing assumptions about lifestyles in later life (e.g., travel versus staying home) can be another point of contention.

Changes in marital relationships can be profound. A *U.S. News and World Report* article notes,

> For some couples, the fact that they have been drifting apart for years could be masked or ignored because most of their time and attention is devoted to their careers or raising a family. For these couples, suddenly spending more time together may present a reality they aren't prepared for. They may find that they no longer have as much in common as they did while they were dating and during the early years of their marriage.

During the past 30 years, the divorce rate of older Americans has roughly tripled. Among older adults who divorced, about a third (34 percent) were married for at least 30 years and 12 percent for 40 years or more. Issues that arise during later life (e.g., out-of-sync beliefs about finances and use of time) are one cause, as are healthier life spans and higher expectations of marriage. Deirdre Bair, author of *The 40-Year Itch*, interviewed 310 people who divorced after long marriages and found consistent themes of opportunity, control, freedom, and independence to explore and pursue personal interests.

Non-spousal family relationships also require transitions. Issues to consider include current and future support for elderly parents and/or adult children, the geographic location of family members, pros (e.g., better weather) and cons (e.g., less frequent contact with family members) of relocation, and expectations with respect to caregiving and childcare services. Sometimes, adult children relocate to be part of a care-giving solution for their parents, and sometimes grandparents relocate to provide a childcare solution for their adult children. Children may need to relocate again for work, however, leaving "trailing grandparents" behind. There are also considerations 20 to 30 years in the future when people who are now in their 60s will become frail elders in their 80s and 90s.

There is evidence that parents' levels of happiness are shaped by their children. One study found that living *near* but not *with* adult children is beneficial. A survey of nearly 2,000 retirees found that those who lived "near or close" to at least half of their children were five times more likely to be happy than those who did not. Like spouses, however, parents with newly minted time availability and their family members need to discuss expectations and set boundaries for "together time." Preferences can range from "We have our own life and babysitting is not part of our plans" to "Sure, we'll watch the kids every day while you are at work."

A final relationship "switch" in later life is maintaining old friendships and making new friends. Studies have found that people with strong social circles live longer and better. Studies have also found that, the older people get, the more challenging it can be to make friends, especially after leaving the workplace, which is a common way people meet. Reasons cited for less social engagement by older adults include busyness with family and work, technology replacing face-to-face interaction, moving far distances, and "forgetting" how to be a friend (i.e., investing time and energy in another person's life).

Forbes writer Robert Laura described later life friendlessness in stark terms:

> "Of course, in retirement you'll have more time and fewer distractions, so you can ideally reconnect then and make up for lost time. But frankly, it may be too late. It's been said that most people only have the capacity to manage 5-10 personal relationships. Therefore, if you don't solidify

your position in relationships that mean the most to you, someone else will."

Translation: casual acquaintances cannot simply morph into close friends just because you have more free time.

- **Share Your Retirement Vision**—Envision your life after work and discuss your ideal lifestyle with family and close friends. For example, discuss any plans to travel for leisure or to visit family members and time you'd like to devote to part-time work or volunteering.

- **Identify Separate and "Together" Activities**—Pursue a mix of shared activities that you and your spouse enjoy doing together and individual activities that you prefer to pursue individually or with others.

- **Cultivate Separate Friends**—Develop a social life apart from your spouse to avoid becoming too dependent on each other and/or having too much togetherness.

- **Create a Personal Space**—Designate a space in your home as a place to be alone or to pursue individual interests guilt-free. "Man caves" and "she-sheds" provide a sanctuary that can reduce "togetherness tension."

- **Be Patient**—Allow time for yourself and your spouse to adjust to life without the structure of a full-time job, experiment with new pursuits (e.g., part-time work or volunteering), and find your way.

- **Get Help When Needed**—Consider marriage counseling if spending more time together is causing frequent disagreements about issues, such as money, lifestyle choices, time use, and family relationships.

- **Define Your Boundaries**—Have honest discussions with family members about your dreams, preferred lifestyle, and the frequency and type of caregiving or other supports that you feel comfortable providing and receiving.

- **Use Tech Tools**—Stay connected with friends and family who do not live nearby. Set a designated day and time to check in with one another. Tech options include Zoom, Skype, Facebook Live, and Apple FaceTime.

- **Go Where People Are**—Consider volunteering or joining community organizations. One of the best ways to build bonds with others is to regularly do meaningful activities together.

- **Be Neighborly**—Get to know people who live near you. Spend time together and build trust through "sharing activities" (e.g., picking up packages, bartering equipment, and neighborhood parties).

- **Make the Time**—Invest the time necessary to build and maintain strong connections with others. Strong relationships are like a two-way street with give and take by both parties.

- **Be Kind**—Make a special effort to be helpful, thoughtful, and kind to others and to compliment them, as appropriate. Acts of kindness can help build and maintain strong relationships with family and friends.

References

Akitunde, A. (2017). How Retirement Can Hurt Your Marriage (And What You Can Do About It). *Huffington Post*. https://www.huffpost.com/entry/divorce-after-50-retirement_n_3286342

Baby Boomers Have Trouble Making New Friends in Retirement, Research Shows (2016). *Chicago Tribune*. http://www.chicagotribune.com/lifestyles/sc-making-friends-older-family-0823-20160819-story.html

Bair, D. (2010). The 40-Year Itch. *The New York Times*. https://www.nytimes.com/2010/06/04/opinion/04bair.html

Breeding, B. (2016). *Is Retiring Where Your Grandchildren Live a Good Move?* myLifeSite. https://www.mylifesite.net/blog/post/is-retiring-where-your-grandchildren-live-a-good-move/

Cohen, P.L. (2018). *Why You Should Consider Moving Away from Your Grown Kids*. Next Avenue. https://www.nextavenue.org/moving-away-grown-kids/

Fischer, J. (2018). An Emotional Playbook for Couples in Retirement. *Forbes*. https://www.forbes.com/sites/nextavenue/2018/06/27/an-emotional-playbook-for-couples-in-retirement/#5b3af33f75ba

Hall, N. (2019). *8 Tips to Survive Your Husband's Retirement*. Verywell Mind. https://www.verywellmind.com/survive-your-husbands-retirement-4021742

Hester, T. (2018). *Hustling Hard for New Friends in Early Retirement*. Our Next Life. https://ournextlife.com/2018/04/16/new-friends-in-early-retirement/

Hughes, D. (2017). 10 Tips to Help Your Marriage Survive Retirement. *U.S. News and World Report*. https://money.usnews.com/money/blogs/

on-retirement/articles/2017-03-30/10-tips-to-help-your-marriage-survive-retirement

Laura, R. (2016). Three Reasons Why You Won't Have Any Friends in Retirement. *Forbes*. https://www.forbes.com/sites/robertlaura/2016/12/21/three-reasons-why-you-wont-have-any-friends-in-retirement/#2b3828f52d1f

Moss, W. (2018). *"Living Near, But Not With, the Kids": And, Other Important Rules for Retirement Happiness*. https://www.yourwealth.com/living-near-but-not-with-the-kids-and-other-important-rules-for-retirement-happiness/

Singletary, M. (2018). Can Retirement Ruin Your Marriage? *The Washington Post*. https://www.washingtonpost.com/news/get-there/wp/2018/05/07/can-retirement-ruin-your-marriage/

The Pitfalls of Too Much Togetherness After Retirement (2019). Still the Lucky Few. https://www.stilltheluckyfew.com/there-are-pitfalls-in-too-much-togetherness-in-marriage-after-retirement/

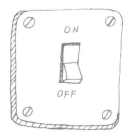

Chapter 18: Becoming the Family Storyteller

One "flipped switch" that can occur before or after leaving a long-term career is becoming the official (or unofficial) storyteller for your family. This often happens when surviving members of the previous generation pass away and you become the executor of their estate or otherwise gain possession of key family historical documents, such as birth and death certificates. You are now the oldest living member of the family and the person who has probably heard family stories the longest.

So, what to do? Well, that's up to you. You have an opportunity—some would say a responsibility—to share your family stories. If you do not do this, it's likely that nobody else will and your ancestors' rich history will be lost forever. Tell stories and assemble supporting documents even if younger generations don't seem interested at the time; they probably will be somewhere down the road. Storyteller Rachael Rifkin notes,

> Most people don't know much about their family history. This is because people usually don't become interested in genealogy until they're in their 50s and 60s, when they have more time to reflect on their family identity. The problem is that by that time, their grandparents and parents have often already passed away or are unable to recount their stories.

Record your recollections and those of parents, grandparents, siblings, cousins, aunts, and uncles before it is too late. It is easy to scan photos and other pieces of physical documentation, and tools like Storyworth, Your

Moments, Your Tribute, and Everlasting Footprint facilitate storytelling through simple group question prompts and/or website development.

Why the emphasis of family storytelling? A growing body of research has found that the single most important thing that can bring families together is to develop a strong family narrative. Specifically, researchers Marshall Duke and Robyn Fivush found the following results: "The more children knew about their family's history, the stronger their sense of control over their lives, the higher their self-esteem and the more successfully they believed their families functioned."

Duke and Fivash used a measurement scale called "The 20 Questions," which included prompts like "Do you know where your mother grew up?" "Do you know where your father grew up?" Do you know where some of your grandparents grew up?" "Do you know where your parents were married?" and "Do you know some of the lessons that your parents learned from good or bad experiences?" Other researchers have found that children who are told family stories tell better stories themselves and have better coping skills.

Psychologists have concluded that people who know a lot about their family history tend to be more resilient and happy. According to these psychologists, there are three types of family stories: "ascending narratives" in which things got better over time (e.g., generation #1 finished eighth grade, generation #2 finished high school, and generation #3 finished college), "descending narratives" in which things got worse (e.g., a "riches to rags" story), and "oscillating narratives" where families have ups and downs (e.g., one family member is a respected community leader and another fell victim to a drug addiction). It is the later category that is particularly effective because these stories teach family members that it is possible to "bounce back" from difficult situations. Especially when accompanied by photos, stories also help younger generations visualize their older relatives as young adults.

A family story that impacted me was one that my mother told me when I was in my late 40s. She explained that my Irish immigrant grandparents made and sold home-made whisky during the Prohibition. Using a recipe from their homeland and a still, they supplied a steady customer base in Woodside, Queens, NYC. The proceeds from their home-based "side hustle" (my grandfather also worked for a railroad) helped them prosper at a time when "No Irish Wanted" discrimination was rampant in the US. As my mother told the story, one customer did not wait to get home to drink the "merchandise," so my grandparents decided to end the business before they got caught. Somewhere in the ground in Woodside are the buried remains of their enterprise. When I told the story to cousins later, they, too, were amazed. Our grandparents were in their late 50s when we were born and always seemed "old" and unassuming to us. They were obviously also amazingly resourceful as young adults.

- **Decide to Be a Storyteller**—Embrace the role and its potential impact on family well-being and pro-actively collect family stories before it is too late. According to researchers from The Family Narratives Lab, knowledge of specific facts is not as important as the process of family members sharing stories about their lives. High scores on the *Do You Know?* (20 Questions) scale were found to be a strong predictor of children's happiness and emotional health.

- **Use Available Resources**—Explore recorded history (e.g., U.S. Census records) using websites such as Ancestry, FindMyPast, and Family Search. Solicit stories from family members using apps such as Storyworth, Footprint, and StoryCatcher Lite that collect written and/or video recorded responses to a bank of starter questions that are then emailed to participants or posted online. There are also companies, like Smitten Films, that create videos of family stories from interviews and photographs.

- **Involve Adult Children and Grandchildren**—Encourage children to interview their parents and grandparents and contribute to family storytelling. One of my family's best insights into my maternal grandmother's life was a letter that she wrote to my cousin's son as data for a school project. The letter describes how she was raised on a farm, came to the US from Ireland at age 17 on a British liner, the Baltic, and arrived in New York City in 1913. In 1918, four members of her family died of the Spanish Flu, to which the COVID-19 coronavirus in 2020 is often compared.

- **Impart Values with Stories**—Incorporate values lessons into family stories, so they have a greater impact beyond simply telling the story itself. Examples include: the value of hard work, the value of post-secondary education, and the value of personal qualities such as helpfulness and honesty.

- **Look for Family Story Parallels**—Listen carefully to younger family members when they share stories about life events and current challenges. Their stories may provide a segue for you to relate their experiences to similar events that you or other family members previously experienced at their age.

- **Provide Historical Context**—Research historical events that occurred around the time of ancestors' lives and share this context along with family stories. Otherwise you run the risk of younger generations misunderstanding past family stories by viewing them with a present-day "lens." I researched Irish immigration and learned that my grandparents were part of a second wave of post-famine Irish immigrants.

- **Build Storytelling into Holiday Celebrations**—Develop a strategy to exchange family stories at holiday gatherings, like Thanksgiving. To get the conversation started, ask family members to bring old family photos, videos, and/or heirlooms and discuss the stories around them.

- **Groom a Successor**—Identify one or more younger family members who are interested in your family history. Ask them to consider becoming the family's next-in-line storyteller. Make sure that they have heard all the family's most treasured stories and have access to family photo albums and written family records.

References

Cooke, L. (2017). *How to Write Family History More Powerfully: Tips from a Master Storyteller.* https://lisalouisecooke.com/2017/05/24/write-family-history-2/

Feller, B. (2013). The Stories That Bind Us. *The New York Times.* https://www.nytimes.com/2013/03/17/fashion/the-family-stories-that-bind-us-this-life.html

Fivush, R. (2016). The "Do You Know?" 20 Questions About Family Stories. *Psychology Today.* https://www.psychologytoday.com/us/blog/the-stories-our-lives/201611/the-do-you-know-20-questions-about-family-stories

Lefkowitz, F. (2013). Start Talking: The Power of Storytelling. *Good Housekeeping.* https://www.goodhousekeeping.com/life/parenting/tips/a19408/power-of-storytelling/

Reese, E. (2013). What kids Learn from Hearing Family Stories. *The Atlantic.* https://www.theatlantic.com/education/archive/2013/12/what-kids-learn-from-hearing-family-stories/282075/

Rifkin, R. (2019). We're Losing Generations of Family History Because We Don't Share our Stories. *Good Housekeeping.* https://www.goodhousekeeping.com/life/a29610101/preserve-family-history-storytelling/

Storyworth: Preserving a Family History, One Story at a Time (2016). Family Search. https://www.familysearch.org/blog/en/storyworth-preserving-family-history-story-time/

Wingate, L. (2015). *Storytelling for Families.* https://lisawingate.com/storytelling-for-families/

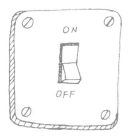

Chapter 19: Successful "Solo Aging"

A major transition that increasing numbers of Americans are facing is "solo aging." This means living alone without the "safety net" of a spouse or children to provide practical, physical, and emotional support during later life. Some people are "solo-agers" for decades if they never married or had children, while others are thrust into this category later on when a spouse predeceases or divorces them or adult children move away or become estranged. Regardless of the timing and circumstances, solo-agers face special challenges, such as the need for support in the event of incapacity, selecting a health care proxy, and assistance with errands, chores, and medical appointments.

Another popular, but somewhat controversial, term used to describe people who are aging alone with little or no social support system is "elder orphans." Single people without children have pushed back against this term, however, claiming that it is inaccurate and stigmatizing. As Bella DePaulo noted in *Psychology Today*, "Orphans are people without parents, they are not adults without children. It trades in the stereotype of older people as child-like and it is pitying."

Regardless of which term is used, many older adults are, or will be (if their spouse pre-deceases them), aging alone. Using public data, Dr. Maria Carney and colleagues estimated that about 22.6 percent of older adults fall into this category or are at risk of doing so in the future. Worse yet, this statistic does not include people with children who are unable or unwilling to take care of them, thus making the actual percentage of solo-agers even higher. Research indicates they are at risk for a variety of negative outcomes, including financial fraud, functional decline, mental-health issues (e.g., depression), and premature death.

Dr. Carney describes solo-agers as "hidden in plain sight right before us," noting that "as independent individuals, they have functioned sufficiently well on their own. As they age and decline, they realize, often too late, that they can no longer complete many of the tasks that they were previously able to do." Government statistics lend support for this concern. US Census data from 2012 showed that about one-third of Americans age 45 to 63 are single—a 50 percent increase from 1980. In addition, about 20 percent of female baby-boomers never had children versus the approximately 10 percent of women in the previous generation. About 1 in 11 Americans age 50 and older lacks a spouse, partner, or living child.

Most experts recommend devoting serious attention to building a surrogate support network and doing so before a health crisis or death of a spouse occurs. *U.S. News and World Report* writer Teresa Mears advised the following: "While you may be able to pay people to help with some tasks, at some point you will still need assistance from people you trust. If you don't have family who will step up, cultivating strong friendships becomes essential. You want to really work hard to have a broad social network."

A great resource to help solo-agers address their unique issues is the "Elder Orphans Aging Alone" group on Facebook. Created in January of 2016 by Robin Young, a solo-ager who provided care for her parents and then wondered "Who will do that for me?", the group had almost 10,000 members in January of 2020. Users have to be age 55 or over, live without a spouse, and either be child-less or have children who are estranged or live far away. Common discussion topics include not being able to rely on caregivers, the health care system's assumption of family support, transportation options, renting rooms to potential caregivers, feelings about not having children, and maintaining a social network while aging.

Of all the "switches" that people face, this is perhaps the most difficult one to flip. You either have a spouse or children or you don't and, if you are married, there is a 50 percent chance that you will eventually be a "solo-ager," perhaps higher if you are female, younger, and/or have better health

HOW TO FLIP

THIS SWITCH

habits than your spouse. What to do? Social science researchers often use a combination of research methods (e.g., surveys, focus groups, observations) called triangulation to study a topic. Similarly, solo-agers need to triangulate by taking as many positive actions as possible to secure a "good ending" for their life. Below are eight suggestions:

- **Expand Your Social Network**—Avoid isolation and loneliness. Make an effort to go where others are. Join organizations, volunteer for non-profit agencies, and attend classes and/or church services for repeated exposure to a group of people. Cultivate relationships with friends (particularly younger ones) with common interests and groups where, like the TV show *Cheers*, "everybody knows your name."

- **Get a Medical Alert Service**—Picture yourself alone at home, or elsewhere, after a fall. Who would you call for help? Suddenly, those television ads for medical alert devices that summon help with the press of a button make sense. Shop around carefully among providers and purchase a monitored alert system. Another option is to arrange daily "well-being checks" with local non-profit agencies.

- **Buddy Up**—Consider sharing a home with other solo-agers (the so-called *Golden Girls* option) by either renting out rooms in your house or moving in with others. Another option is for one or more solo-agers to provide free live-in housing for a caregiver who provides assistance with activities of daily living.

- **Lean on Professionals**—Find out how much support is possible from an elder law attorney, financial planner, CPA, or others in the event of a health crisis, frailty, or other issue. Some professionals may be willing to assist in some capacity as surrogates for non-existent family members. Others will consider this beyond the scope of their services or avoid doing so because they are already helping aging parents.

- **Consider a CCRC**—Shop around for a continuing care retirement community (CCRC) that provides lifetime care as you get older. Do this well in advance of a health crisis and move in when you can still live independently. You will need significant savings, however, or assets (e.g., a house) that can be liquidated. Entry fees for CCRCs range from about $200,000 to $500,000 and monthly fees from about $2,000 to $4,000 on average.

- **Live in a 55+ Community**—Move to a place where there are ample opportunities to meet people, join group activities, and avoid social isolation. Many developments offer a sense of community, convenient locations for transportation services, numerous amenities (e.g., pool and fitness center) and support services (e.g., snow plowing), and safety and security features (e.g., guard gates and well-lit common areas).

- **Get Your Affairs in Order**—Prepare a will, living will, and durable power of attorney. Ask your attorney for advice if it is difficult to name people for key positions, such as executor and health care proxy. Financial institutions, such as banks and estate planning attorneys, can also serve as executors. Also have a long-term care (LTC) plan, which may include a LTC insurance policy or savings to self-insure.

- **Live a Healthy Lifestyle**—Eat healthy food, avoid smoking, and get adequate sleep, daily physical activity, and routine health-screening exams. Do everything humanly possible to stave off, or at least postpone, chronic diseases like heart disease, cancer, and diabetes. For optimum mental health, connect with others, do things you enjoy, and have a sense of purpose in your life.

References

Adamy, J. & Overberg, P. (2018). More Than Ever, Americans Age Alone. *The Wall Street Journal.* https://www.wsj.com/articles/the-loneliest-generation-americans-more-than-ever-are-aging-alone-11544541134

Aging Baby Boomers, Childless and Unmarried, at Risk of Becoming 'Elder Orphans.' (2015). *Science Daily.* https://www.sciencedaily.com/releases/2015/05/150515083532.htm

Carny, M.T., Fujiwara, J., Emmert, B.E., Liberman, T.A. & Paris, B. (2016). Elder Orphans Hiding in Plain Sight: A Growing Vulnerable Population. *Current Gerontology and Geriatrics Research.* https://www.ncbi.nlm.nih.gov/pmc/articles/PMC5097795/

DePaulo, B. (2016). Elder Orphans: A Real Problem or a New Way to Scare Singles? *Psychology Today.* https://www.psychologytoday.com/us/blog/living-single/201610/elder-orphans-real-problem-or-new-way-scare-singles

'Elder Orphans' Facebook Group Creates Community for Adults Aging Alone (2017). WBUR. https://www.wbur.org/hereandnow/2017/08/15/elder-orphans

Graham, J. (2018). 'Elder Orphans,' Without kids or Spouses, face old Age Alone. *The Washington Post.* https://www.washingtonpost.com/national/health-science/elder-orphans-without-kids-or-spouses-face-old-age-alone/2018/10/12/a2c9384a-cb24-11e8-a3e6-44daa3d35ede_story.html

Mears, T. (2016). *How to Plan for Aging if You're an 'Elder Orphan.'* Yahoo News: https://www.yahoo.com/news/plan-aging-youre-elder-orphan-190315525.html

Ray, M. (2012). *Baby Boomers Without Kids face Uncertainty in Senior Years.* Sunrise Senior Living. https://www.sunriseseniorliving.com/blog/

november-2012/baby-boomers-without-kids-face-uncertainty-in-senior-years.aspx

Weston, L. (2019). Three Steps to Keep 'Solo Agers' Happier and Safer. *Nerd Wallet*. https://apnews.com/bde20288b84745bc9173ebee1ef057d3

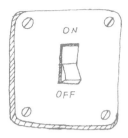

Chapter 20: Finding Meaning and Purpose with Others

What is the secret to happiness and success in later life? Internationally known author, speaker, and actuary Anna Rappaport developed the concept of *The Life Portfolio*, which, like a portfolio of investments, requires diversification and ongoing management. *The Life Portfolio* includes four essential components:

- **Health**—Activities related to health maintenance and support services

- **People**—Relationships with family, friends, organizations, and new contacts

- **Pursuits**—Activities, such as work, volunteering, hobbies, community events, caregiving, and travel

- **Places**—Ties to a home and community, as well as travel destinations

Even when people are comfortable financially, a gap in any of these areas can lead to unhappiness, boredom, loneliness, and/or lack of fulfillment. While ample savings and financial security support each part of *The Life Portfolio*, it is not about money. Rappaport notes, "A simple way of deciding if things are working out is to periodically (at least once a year) think about what one has been doing. If you are doing things that you are happy about and proud of, then I would call that success."

Previous chapters noted that, when workplace social connections cease, it is important to build new social capital (i.e., relationships with tangible and intangible benefits) in later life, especially for solo-agers. This means not just showing up randomly to places or events but being there on a regular basis to build personal connections with others. Below are six key benefits of socialization:

- **Belongingness**—Feeling that you "fit in" when you are around people with similar interests and beliefs

- **Self-Worth**—Feeling valuable and connected through positive interactions with others

- **Mental Health**—Fostering positive feelings by being with people and doing fun or rewarding activities

- **Cognition**—Exercising your brain through conversation and interaction with others

- **Purposefulness**—Doing meaningful things with others provides something to look forward to each day

- **Longevity**—Being socially active can result in a longer lifespan when compared to living in a state of isolation, which poses health risks

People are happier and more satisfied with some scheduled activities in their lives. Fortunately, there are many places and activities that can provide enjoyment, fulfillment, and/or socialization. A review of the book *Life Starts at Retirement* and online references uncovered the following suggestions:

- **Continuing Education**—Arts and crafts programs, classes, conferences, expos, and lectures

- **Events**—Concerts, fairs, festivals, holiday celebrations, parades, and sporting events

150

- **Games**—Board games (e.g., Monopoly), card games, and video games

- **Organizations**—Alumni groups, boards of non-profit organizations, book clubs, card clubs, choirs, gardening clubs, lunch date groups, political groups, and sports clubs (e.g., bowling leagues)

- **Physical Activity**—Group exercise classes (e.g., Zumba), gyms, and walking groups

- **Public Spaces**—Camping, dog parks, libraries, movies, museums, state and national parks, and theaters

Apart from paid employment, there is perhaps no better way to meet people on a recurring basis, build relationships, and do meaningful work than to volunteer for a local organization or non-profit agency. Other benefits include having fun, gaining the satisfaction of making a difference, and learning new skills. Studies have also found that volunteering has physical and mental health benefits, such as lower mortality and depression rates, better functional ability and health, reduced risk for Alzheimer's disease, and lower stress levels. Another benefit is that volunteering makes people feel "time affluent," meaning they feel like they have more time. This is like studies that have found that people feel wealthier when they donate money to charity. In both situations, there is personal satisfaction achieved when people are not wasting assets (time and money) or spending them only on themselves.

HOW TO FLIP THIS SWITCH

- **Start Early**—Work on pieces of *The Life Portfolio* (e.g., health maintenance, relationships, pursuits) well before leaving full-time work. Anna Rappaport notes, "My view is that it is better to start on this before retirement and to have some pieces of a life portfolio in place, or ready to be put in place quickly."

- **Give Yourself a Pep Talk**—Repeat the following mantra daily: "I am moving on to the next chapter of my life. I have plenty of knowledge and skills to offer others. I can contribute value to people and/or organizations. Being with and helping others is good for me."

- **Take Time to Evolve**—Give yourself time to develop a new post-career lifestyle. It is not like an "on-off" switch for most people but, rather, a series of transitions over many years. Focus on developing new relationships, new communities, and new sources of joy, hope, and meaning after paid employment ends.

- **Live Purposefully**—Begin with the end in mind: your vision of a desired lifestyle in later life. Then develop goals and action steps that support your vision. For example, if you want to do volunteer work, initial action steps might include researching nearby volunteer opportunities and lining up character references.

- **Get Social**—Take advantage of "bonding resources" that social media provides. One example is online groups for people with like interests as depicted in the television advertisement showing a Facebook-enabled meet up of basset hound owners. Another resource is tools like Skype, Zoom, Facebook video, or FaceTime for conversations.

- **Stay Connected**—If you were involved in a professional or trade association throughout your full-time working career, remain a member for socialization and volunteer or paid-employment opportunities. Remember that just because you leave a job, it does not mean that you must leave a job-related professional association. Some groups have life member or emeritus dues rates for older members.

- **Become a Volunteer**—Pick a non-profit organization that does work that you support and/or has volunteer roles that are fun and/or fit your skill set. Contact the agency and apply to become a volunteer or board member. Be prepared to have to complete an application, be interviewed, provide character references, and have a background check and/or credit check just as if you were applying for employment.

- **Become a Joiner**—Look around your community for organizations and activities that interest you and reach out to get involved. Review their websites first to get a feel for each organization's culture and policies and to learn the names of its elected leaders.

- **Go Public**—Look for opportunities to meet and connect with people in public places such as dog parks, dog walking groups, libraries, churches, and coffee shops. Another option is meet-ups. To find groups of like-minded individuals in your area, visit www.MeetUp.com and search for events in your town or county.

- **Be Picky**—Use caution with initial decisions and time commitments. Don't book every free minute or get involved in multiple activities too quickly. Plan to do activities (e.g., travel) that are physically demanding while you can because you may not be mobile—and they may not be feasible—in later years.

References

8 Long-Term Benefits of Volunteering (2017). Nonprofit Hub. https://nonprofithub.org/featured/8-long-term-health-benefits-of-volunteering/

11 Life-Changing Benefits of Volunteering That May Not Be So Obvious (2017). BUILD Abroad. https://buildabroad.org/2017/09/01/benefits-of-volunteering/

5 Surprising Benefits of Volunteering (2015). *Forbes.* https://www.forbes.com/sites/nextavenue/2015/03/19/5-surprising-benefits-of-volunteering/#6766d1d3127b

Fritz, J. (2019). *15 Unexpected Benefits of Volunteering That Will Inspire You* (2019). The Balance. https://www.thebalancesmb.com/unexpected-benefits-of-volunteering-4132453

Harry, L. (2017). *Life Starts at Retirement.* Appleseed Press Book Publishers, LLC.

Not Just BINGO: Meaningful Activities for Older Adults. Jenerations Health. https://jenerationshealth.com/not-just-bingo-meaningful-activities-for-older-adults/

Participating in Activities You Enjoy (2017). National Institute on Aging. https://www.nia.nih.gov/health/participating-activities-you-enjoy

Pollock, K. (2016). *Beyond Bingo: 14 Activities for Elderly People That Aren't Boring.* The Arbor Company Senior Living Blog. https://blog.arborcompany.com/14-activities-for-elderly-people-that-arent-boring

Rappaport, A. (2019). *Reboot, Rewire or Retire? Personal Experiences with Phased Retirement and Managing a Life Portfolio.* Nerd's Eye View. https://

www.kitces.com/blog/anna-rappaport-phased-retirement-life-portfolio-health-people-pursuits-places/

Reibstein, D.L. (2017). *How Staying Social Benefits Seniors.* 55Living.com: http://www.55living.com/blog/how-staying-social-benefits-seniors.html

The Importance of Socializing for Seniors (2017). Acts Retirement Life Communities. https://www.actsretirement.org/latest-retirement-news/blog/2017/12/12/the-importance-of-socializing-for-seniors/

Volunteering and Its Surprising Benefits (2019). Help Guide. https://www.helpguide.org/articles/healthy-living/volunteering-and-its-surprising-benefits.htm

PART 3: Lifestyle Transitions

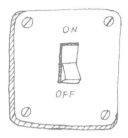

Chapter 21: FINDing Fulfillment
After Full-Time Work

In Chapter 2, the FIRE (Financial Independence, Retire Early) movement was described. However, many people who espouse FIRE and exit the labor force in mid-life still work in some capacity as sole proprietors or independent contractors. For example, FIRE enthusiast, Mr. Money Mustache, has a revenue-producing blog and other income sources in addition to the $600,000 portfolio that he accumulated when he left a software engineer job at age 30. As post-retirement expert, Anna Rappaport, notes, "One cannot be on vacation all of the time. Vacation is a break from what we normally do. People who retire with the idea of an endless vacation are likely to be disappointed or bored within a year or two, if not sooner."

The traditional definition of retirement is "leaving one's job and ceasing to work." A better acronym than FIRE for post-work life—at any age—is FIND (**F**inancial **I**ndependence, **N**ew **D**irections). By avoiding the "R" word, FIND encompasses many possible life options—whether it occurs at ages 30 to 45 or 55 to 70 (or later). Unlike FIRE, FIND does not imply the end of your working career. Rather, it simply means that you have the freedom to live your best possible life on your own terms. FINDing yourself is a major flipped switch with **N**ew **D**irections that include continued full-time work, part-time work, self-employment, freelancing, no work, volunteering, full-time (e.g., five days) or part-time (e.g., two days) family caregiving, travel, and more.

By 2026, an estimated 30 percent of Americans age 65 to 74 will be working compared to about 17 percent in 1996. Older adults who intend to remain employed or become self-employed must control their personal narrative, lest others assume that they are no longer productive or relevant and are focused on a life of leisure. Create a vision of who you want to be and develop a plan to reinvent yourself. Suggested strategies for older workers include: avoiding the "R" word as a self-description, dressing appropriately for a work location (e.g., business casual in many workplaces), using social media to brand and market yourself, building and maintaining professional contacts, and continuing professional development in both your area of expertise and technology. To do otherwise is to risk subtle, and sometimes very overt, ageism. Witness "Okay, Boomer," the snarky phrase that exploded in 2019 to indicate that an older person is hopelessly obtuse and out of date.

It is not easy to switch off a professional career. Rather, it is quite common for people to scale back their work activities over time. Anna Rappaport notes, "People in senior management or professional roles often want a period of professional activity of their choosing before totally leaving such roles." Similar sentiments were expressed by several of my former colleagues. One described her desire for a "real retirement" after seven years of post-career entrepreneurship, saying, "I just don't want to do it [freelance work] anymore." Another noted that, after 13 years of post-career freelancing, "My one regular gig providing trainings for building code officials ended when my seminars covered all the training venues around the state. While I would likely accept any new offers, I think that now I am officially retired. Still keeping busy though."

People who become entrepreneurs or freelancers after decades of working for others need to develop a value proposition and project management skills. Start by asking "What work deliverables can I provide that create value for others?" and "What is the value of my time and the market value for services like those that I will be providing?" Next, develop a business plan that includes the following sections: Executive Summary, Business Overview, Market Analysis, Competitive Analysis, Marketing Plan, Operating Plan, and Financial Projections. Dozens of business-plan template forms can be found online. Finally, develop a plan for "juggling" multiple assignments. Ideally, have some clients and work projects lined up via side hustles before leaving a long-time career.

When someone stops working, they have about 2,500 extra hours a year to fill (50 hours of work/commuting time x 50 weeks, assuming a two-week vacation previously). Roughing out a daily time schedule can help manage this newfound time. Whatever your **New Directions** are, be cautious about over-committing to a job, freelance work, volunteer roles, and caregiving. Don't book every minute. Taking on the time equivalent of a new full-time job can be overwhelming and eat up valuable time that may be better spent building and maintaining relationships. It is perfectly fine to say no to requests that are not a good fit for your skill set, passions, interests, or time constraints. You can't do everything, and the choices that you make have opportunity costs.

- **Leave Work with a Plan**—Anticipate your next act. Print business cards and develop a website for future freelance work and line up future work or volunteer opportunities. The same goes for travel plans. A seamless transition from work to your **New Direction** will provide daily structure and a sense of purpose, whatever it may be.

- **Don't Disappear for Long**—A 2019 study found the average retiree grows bored after just one year of post-work life. One in ten struggle to find daily pastimes after just five months! A colleague told me he was advised to return to the labor force within two years of when he stepped away from a long-time job on Wall Street, or he would be deemed "rusty" and irrelevant. He did just that and currently runs a thriving non-profit financial education organization in New Jersey, his "second act."

- **Phase Out Gradually**—Explore a phased transition from full-time work to fewer hours and/or less responsibility. Often, instead of having a formal policy, employers make "deals" with older workers on a case-by-case basis. Be sure to review the impact phasing out might have on any pension or Social Security benefits you might have available.

- **Do Work You Like**—Colleagues have told me that they cherry-picked features of former jobs to continue in some capacity and let the rest go. A former administrator writes articles for her local newspaper, and a former academic started a copy-editing business to help professors polish their journal article manuscripts.

- **Find Resources**—Reach out for help when it is needed. For example, you will need a source of technical support when employer IT resources end. Organizations, such as the Small Business Administration, SCORE, and a local Chamber of Commerce, can assist with business development.

- **Expect Ageism**—According to AARP, about 3 in 5 older workers have seen or experienced workplace age discrimination. While there is no magic bullet to avoid it, a current skillset, well-developed list of professional contacts, recent significant achievements, trendy clothing, and—yes—even hair dye can help.

- **Expect Future Changes**—Anticipate changes in New Directions over time. For example, work may not seem as important—or be as available—a decade out from a long-time career, or it could be precluded by illness, injury, infirmity, or family caregiving roles.

References

Adeney, P. (2018). *Mr. Money Mustache says Suze Orman Has it Wrong on Financial Independence and Early Retirement.* Marketwatch. https://www.marketwatch.com/story/mr-money-mustache-wants-suze-orman-and-everyone-else-to-understand-these-8-things-about-the-fire-movement-2018-10-05

Getting Closer to Retirement (n.d.). Investor Protection Trust. http://www.investorprotection.org/downloads/IPT_WI65_Getting_Closer_to_Retirement_Action_Guide.pdf

Hannon, K. (2019). *Why Working Has Become the New Retirement.* Marketwatch.

Kita, J. (2020). Ageism in the Workplace: It's Time to End the Last Acceptable Bias. *AARP Bulletin*, 61(1), 13-21. https://www.aarp.org/work/working-at-50-plus/info-2019/age-discrimination-in-america.html

Lake, R. (2019). *Is Working in Retirement Worth It?* Yahoo! Finance. https://finance.yahoo.com/news/working-retirement-worth-125500147.html

Macleod, A. (2019). *Is 'OK Boomer' the 'New N-Word,' or Are Millennials Still Destroying Everything?* FAIR. https://fair.org/home/is-ok-boomer-the-new-n-word-or-are-millennials-still-destroying-everything/

Mr. Money Mustache (2020). Wikipedia. https://en.wikipedia.org/wiki/Mr._Money_Mustache

Rappaport, A. (2019). *Reboot, Rewire or Retire? Personal Experiences with Phased Retirement and Managing a Life Portfolio.* Nerd's Eye View. https://www.kitces.com/blog/anna-rappaport-phased-retirement-life-portfolio-health-people-pursuits-places/

Renner, B. (2019). *Retirement Blues: Average Retiree Grows Bored After Just One Year, Survey Finds.* Study Finds. https://www.studyfinds.org/most-people-grow-bored-retirement-just-one-year/

Romano, A. (2019). *"OK Boomer" Isn't Just About the Past. It's About Our Apocalyptic Future.* Vox. https://www.vox.com/2019/11/19/20963757/what-is-ok-boomer-meme-about-meaning-gen-z-millennials

Ward, S. (2019). *How to Write a Business Plan Step by Step.* The Balance. https://www.thebalancesmb.com/business-plan-outline-2947032

What is Retirement? (2019). Investopedia. https://www.investopedia.com/terms/r/retirement.asp

Write Your Business Plan (n.d.). U.S. Small Business Administration. https://www.sba.gov/business-guide/plan-your-business/write-your-business-plan

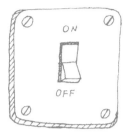

Chapter 22: Downsizing and Divesting

Two switches that many people undertake one or more times in later life are downsizing their living space (e.g., moving from a house to a condominium or apartment) and divesting (i.e., selling, gifting, donating, or throwing away) personal property. Typically, these transitions are linked to major life changes:

- Leaving a job and no longer being tied to a specific geographic location

- Making a long-distance, interstate move (e.g., from Michigan to Florida)

- Entering an assisted-living unit or continuing-care retirement community

- Experiencing a health crisis, disability, or death (e.g., widowhood)

- Having the experience of "cleaning out" parents' houses following their death

Perhaps the hardest part of downsizing is getting started. Fortunately, organizing experts have some very solid advice. Jamie Novak, author of *Keep This, Toss That: The Practical Guide to Tidying Up,* recommends a "small steps" 10-10-10 approach to organization. Set a timer for 10 minutes to find 10 items to share, sell, donate, or toss. Repeat for 10 consecutive days for a total discard of 100 items. Repeat as needed or ramp up as desired (e.g., 20 minutes to divest 20 items for 20 consecutive days = 400 items). Novak also recommends making digital copies of your most treasured items before discarding them and repeating her definition of "CUTE" when you are tempted to "save" items of dubious value: "**Can't. Use. This. Ever.**" Several colleagues told me that they planned to do this with wooden and acrylic plaques that they had collected over the decades for professional awards: photograph them, save the photo files in a folder on their computer, and toss the plaques, so their children would not have to throw them out later.

Marie Kondo, Japanese organizer, author, and star of the hit Netflix show *Tidying Up with Marie Kondo,* has a different take on downsizing. Her philosophy is encouraging people to keep only possessions that "spark joy." Other items must go after thanking them for serving their purpose. Her organizing philosophy is to systematically tackle entire categories of "stuff" (e.g., books, clothing, and kitchen tools) by spreading them out together on the floor, touching them one by one, and keeping only the "joyful" items. By putting similar types of items in a pile, people can see how much they have of each item, which makes the process of prioritizing joy-sparking items easier.

With stock investing, the mantra to make a profit is "Buy Low, Sell High." When downsizing your home, it is "Sell High, Buy Low," so the difference (i.e., capital gain after sales expenses minus the cost of a new dwelling) becomes a source of income. In addition, a smaller home is likely to have lower property taxes, utility bills, and/or maintenance costs. Unfortunately, there is some recent evidence that the "difference" is smaller than many people anticipated. According to the National Association of Realtors, homeowners aged 65 to 74 who downsized, on average, sold a house for $270,000 and bought one for $250,000. A spokesperson noted that older downsizers are competing in the same market for lower-priced homes as younger first-time homebuyers; "All generations are purchasing similar types and sizes of homes."

Divesting possessions also requires reasonable expectations. Items should generally be priced at their current (depreciated) value—not what you paid for them. They will eventually be worth what someone will pay to take them off your hands. Potential sales venues for discarded items include garage/yard sales, consignment shops, newspaper advertising, eBay, Craigslist, and Facebook Marketplace. Be prepared for emotional responses to the "weeding out" process (e.g., thinking about the past and/or the final part of your life).

- **Set Goals**—Develop a strategy to "pare down," whether it is "10 minutes-10 items-10 days," as Jamie Novak suggests, or cleaning out closets or rooms by a certain date. Prepare a "battle plan" of all required tasks and post goals visibly (e.g., on the door of rooms being de-cluttered) for motivation to stay on task.

- **Start Early**—Know that downsizing takes time. One garage sale or Facebook post will not make all your possessions disappear. Schedule sales early and often (I had about 30 garage sales over two summers). Also make timely arrangements for moving services, address changes, donations, and other related tasks.

- **Approach Potential Donees**—Start the divesting process with people you know. Ask friends and family if they are interested in taking any of your discarded items and give them a firm date to pick it up. If that date passes and you still have those items, move on to Plans B (selling), C (donating), and D (trashing).

- **Empty "Extra" Rooms**—Remove items in rooms that you will not have in a new dwelling or make plans to relocate them to the space that you will have in your future home. Examples include items in a garage or a third bedroom. Don't cram "stuff" from a 2,500 square foot home into a 1,400 square foot condo.

- **Make Only Two Piles**—Sort possessions into two piles: "Keep" and "Discard." Experts caution against making a "Maybe" pile because it is likely to be larger than the other two, and you will essentially just have moved possessions to another location.

- **Divest Duplicates**—Follow Marie Kondo's suggestion of grouping similar items together on a table or on the floor. Then do a side-by-side comparison of these items, keep the best, and discard the rest. For example, keep three or four tablecloths if you have 12 and two cookie sheets if you have seven.

- **Professionalize Your Garage (Yard) Sales**—Group like items (e.g., small appliances) and like prices ($1 table, $3 table, etc.) together to make shopping easy for customers. Have plenty of change on hand and good signage. Participate in community-wide garage sales and online advertisements for garage sales, such as Facebook Marketplace.

- **Support Local Charities**—Find thrift shops in your community using *The Thrift Shopper* website (http://www.thethriftshopper.com/). Simply enter your zip code or city and state and a list will pop up with the name, address, phone number, and a map showing the location of the thrift shop. Check with thrift shops first about what they do or do not take before showing up with a pile of discarded items.

- **Follow the "Three Year Rule"**—Identify the last time that you used "undecided" items (if you can). If it has been at least three years, they are good candidates for divesting. One de-cluttering and organizing expert, Donna Smallin, author of *Simple Steps to Organizing Everything*, recommends placing hard-to-pitch items in a box with an "open by" date a year in the future. If the box is still unopened at the one-year date, pitch it.

- **Get Help, If Needed**—Pay professional helpers if the downsizing and/or moving process seems daunting. Contact the National Association of Senior Move Managers (www.nasmm.org) to find a local moving specialist and/or professional eBay consignment sellers who sell people's items for a commission (e.g., 10 percent of an item's sale price)

References

A Guide to Downsizing for Seniors (2020). Senior Living. https://www.seniorliving.org/housing/downsizing/

Coughlin, K. (2019). *Jamie Novak Shares De-Cluttering Tips…and a Dark Secret, in Morristown* (2019). Morristown Green. https://morristowngreen.com/2019/01/30/jamie-novak-shares-de-cluttering-tips-and-a-dark-secret-in-morristown/

Downsizing in Retirement (n.d.). Life Enriching Communities. https://lec.org/blog/downsizing-in-retirement/

Edleson, H. (2015). Downsizing Offers a Fresh Start for Older Adults. *The New York Times*. https://www.nytimes.com/2015/10/03/your-money/downsizing-offers-a-fresh-start-for-older-adults.html

Hart, D. (2019). *Downsizing Paralysis? Empowering Breakthroughs!* Montgomery Place. https://montgomeryplace.org/downsizing-paralysis/

Lowe, Lindsay (2019). *The 'Marie Kondo Effect'? Thrift Store Nationwide See an Uptick in Donations*. Today. https://www.today.com/home/marie-kondo-effect-thrift-stores-nationwide-see-uptick-donations-t146810

Marie Kondo Wants Us to Thank Our Belongings. But Does It Really Help? (2019, January 30). *The Huffington Post*. https://huffpost.com/entry/marie-kondo-saying-thank-you

O'Brien, S. (2018). *Older Americans Planning to Downsize Should Brace for Sticker Shock*. CNBC. https://www.cnbc.com/2018/06/15/older-americans-planning-to-downsize-should-brace-for-sticker-shock.html

Senior-Friendly Guide to Downsizing (2019). MyMove. https://www.mymove.com/moving/senior-guide-downsizing/

Thrift Stores Say They're Swamped with Donations After 'Tidying Up with Marie Kondo' (2019). NPR. https://www.npr.org/2019/01/21/687255642/thrift-stores-say-theyre-swamped-with-donations-after-tidying-up-with-marie-kond

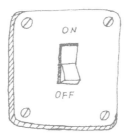

Chapter 23: Getting Help When Needed

A mistake that many older adults make when they first retire is assuming that their life will always look the way it does today. Unfortunately, this is often not the case. Not everyone is healthy or mobile in their later years or can perform the same routine tasks they did when they were younger. You may also simply decide that you can afford to pay someone to do things that you dislike (e.g., cleaning bathroom soap scum or emptying the gutters). It is at these times that former "do it yourselfers" flip a switch from "doing" to "hiring." Examples of functions than are often outsourced include making complex financial decisions, handling asset management, performing house cleaning and maintenance, doing yard work, paying bills, and administering transportation services when someone is unwilling (e.g., night driving) or unable to drive. You may also need IT help since you can no longer pick the brains of the tech whizzes at your former employer.

At no point in life are your finances more complex than age 60 and beyond. There are more issues to address than younger years including: when to claim Social Security, required minimum distributions, Medicare and supplemental insurance, long-term care planning, serious estate planning, and—for prodigious savers—wealth management. In addition, many later life events have financial implications including "gray divorces," widowhood, remarriage, and lump sum distributions from a long-time employer. Some people also just want to ensure that they are on the right track. These are times when hiring a financial advisor can be beneficial.

Hiring a financial advisor requires time to search and screen for someone who is well qualified, experienced, and affordable. When this is done in a crisis (e.g., following the death of a spouse), people often "settle" instead of choosing wisely. Therefore, it makes sense to make arrangements before a crisis occurs. Consider the following factors when selecting a financial advisor:

- **Personal Needs**—Determine the financial services you're in need of. For example, do you need ongoing portfolio management or just a one-time review of your personal finances? Make a list of your financial questions and "issues" to determine what products and services you are looking for.

- **Professional Credentials**—Check out the credentials, licenses, and educational background of financial professionals that you are considering. Look for designations that indicate successful completion of specialized training courses. An example is the CFP® (certified financial planner®) credential.

- **Experience**—Look for someone who has worked in the financial services industry for a while. Practical "real world" experience is as important as designations earned through self-study and exams. Find an advisor who has steered clients through both rising (bull) markets and bear market downturns.

- **Ethics Violations**—Check for information about infractions in an advisor's past through the CFP Board, a state Bureau of Securities, the U.S. Securities and Exchange Commission, or by simply searching advisors' names online. Information might pop up if their misdeeds were reported in local newspapers.

- **Compensation Method**—Ask how a financial advisor is compensated by clients. Typical methods include flat fees (e.g., an hourly rate for services), assets under management fees (e.g., 1 percent of a client's investment value), commissions for the sale of products, or a combination of fees and commissions.

- **Conflicts of Interest**—Find out what conflicts of interest exist, if any. Examples are rewards received by advisors for selling certain investments and business interests in affiliated products or organizations.

Similar "due diligence" is needed to hire helpers for house cleaning, lawn care, and other tasks. Start by asking family and friends if they have any recommendations for companies or self-employed individuals. Check at least three references and contact a local consumer affairs agency, Better Business Bureau, or online referral site, like Angie's List, to see if there are any complaints filed against potential hires. If you are hiring a company, ask for proof that they have done background checks on their employees.

You will need to pay employment (a.k.a., nanny) tax for the employer's share of employee Social Security and Medicare taxes if you hire a house-cleaner or landscaper directly and pay them more than $2,200 in 2020. Also make sure that any service provider that you hire has adequate liability insurance in case someone is injured or property is damaged. Finally, follow the "Rule of Three" and compare at least three service providers. Use the following worksheet to compare features of each firm.

Rule of Three Worksheet for Comparison Shopping

1. Find three comparable products or services from three different sources (e.g. stores and online).

2. Determine the most important product or service features to you in making a purchase and list them in column 1.

3. Compare the three products or services by completing the chart below to list key features of each one.

4. Determine which product or service (of the three) is best for you and explain why.

Name of Product:_____

Product or Service Feature	Vendor #1	Vendor #2	Vendor #3
Price			

The best product or service for me is Vendor #_____ because _____

_____

- **Hire a Financial Planner**—Search these websites to find names, background, and contact information for at least three local financial advisors to interview and compare:

  - CFP Board: https://www.cfp.net/
  - Financial Planning Association (FPA Planner Search): http://www.plannersearch.org/
  - Garrett Planning Network: https://garrettplanningnetwork.com/

- National Association of Personal Financial Advisors (NAPFA): https://www.napfa.org/
- XY Planning Network (XYPN): https://www.xyplanningnetwork. com/

- **Find Free Local Financial Resources**—Look around for help. Some libraries, FPA chapters, and media outlets offer free or low-cost Financial Planning Day events with seminars and exhibits by local advisors. Some large cities offer financial counseling services through Financial Empowerment Centers. Other free financial information and/or advice services include AARP Foundation Tax-Aide, Tax Counseling for the Elderly (TCE), Cooperative Extension, and local area agencies on aging, which often sponsor seminars or pro-bono financial counseling services.

- **Meet Your Legal Obligations**—Take steps to comply with federal and state laws if you hire an individual to work for you as an employee. For example, you may need to confirm an employee's legal work status, as well as withhold and pay taxes. A much simpler arrangement is to hire a service company.

- **Talk Before You Hire**—Interview people who will be working at your home. Ask about their rates and whether they charge by the hour or home/yard size and whether they offer free at-home estimates. Establish clear expectations about frequency of tasks, moving items for cleaning, "off-limits" areas, etc.

- **Lock Down Your House**—Place jewelry, check books, financial records, purses, wallets, and other valuables in a safe, locked file cabinet, or other secure place when household workers are present. Doing this will prevent these items from being misplaced, damaged, or stolen.

- **Go with Your Gut**—Find service providers who take the time to listen to your concerns and those you like and trust. When several service providers are equally competent, choose those with whom you feel most comfortable.

References

Angie's List Tips for Hiring House Cleaning Services (2020). https://www.angieslist.com/articles/angies-list-tips-hiring-house-cleaning-services.htm

AuWerter, S. (2018). Financial Planners for the Rest of Us. *AARP The Magazine*, 61(6c), 24-26. https://www.aarp.org/money/investing/info-2018/find-a-financial-planner.html

Becker, M. (2019). *Six Times You Should Hire a Financial Planner (and Three Times You Shouldn't.* The Simple Dollar. https://www.thesimpledollar.com/investing/retirement/six-times-you-should-hire-a-financial-planner-and-three-times-you-shouldnt/

Eisenhower, N.D. & Petraeus, H. (2013*). Know Your Financial Adviser.* Washington, DC: Consumer Financial Protection Bureau. https://www.consumerfinance.gov/about-us/blog/know-your-financial-adviser/

Francavilla, W. (2018, Sept.). Advice on Evaluating an Adviser from an Industry Veteran. *AAII Journal*, 12-16. https://www.aaii.com/journal/article/advice-on-evaluating-an-adviser-from-an-industry-veteran

Hicks, K. (2018). *5 Tips to Find a Financial Advisor for Seniors.* SeniorAdvisor.com. https://www.senioradvisor.com/blog/2018/01/tips-to-find-a-financial-advisor-for-seniors/

Johnson, S. (n.d.). *The Right Way to Hire Domestic Help.* https://www.legalzoom.com/articles/the-right-way-to-hire-domestic-help

Know Your Financial Adviser. (2013). Washington, DC: Consumer Financial Protection Bureau. https://files.consumerfinance.gov/f/201311_cfpb_flyer_senior-financial-advisors.pdf

Murray, J. (2019). *Hiring and Paying a Household Employee.* The Balance. https://www.thebalancesmb.com/hiring-and-paying-a-household-employee-398606

Nanny Tax Threshold Increases for 2020 (2019). GTM Payroll Services. https://gtm.com/household/nanny-tax-threshold-increases-for-2020/

O'Neill, B. (2018). *How to Select a Financial Advisor* (2018). Rutgers Cooperative Extension. https://njaes.rutgers.edu/sshw/message/message.php?p=Finance&m=383

Quinn. J.B. (2017). Managing Your Manager. *AARP Bulletin*, 58(3), 12.

Segal, T. (2019). When Should You Hire a Financial Advisor? *Investopedia.* https://www.investopedia.com/managing-wealth/when-should-you-hire-financial-advisor/

Sollitto, M. (2020). *In-Home Services That Can Help Seniors Continue to Live Independently.* Aging Care. https://www.agingcare.com/articles/kinds-of-home-care-available-for-seniors-137919.htm

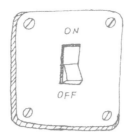

Chapter 24: Disengaging the Past and Engaging the Future

Disengaging from decades of work to do what comes next is not easy. Many people find it hard to let go of their professional life and everything that it encompassed (e.g., structure, authority, income, influence, travel opportunities). Many people report feeling lost and disoriented. In the book *Transitions: Making Sense of Life's Changes*, author William Bridges discusses three stages associated with transitions: an ending phase (disengagement from previously high-priority activities and determining what aspects of a former role to keep and let go of), a neutral phase (a period of unknown changes, confusion, stress, and/or reorientation in between someone's old reality and new identity), and a new beginning phase (engagement with new roles and activities reflecting comfort with a new identity).

Like "senioritis" in high school, the year or two immediately before you exit a long-time career can be a period of increasing mental disengagement. Not surprisingly, there are dozens of articles online with tips for managers who want to keep their late-career employees productive. "Short timers" who don't need to "lean in" anymore because they won't be around to finish projects or receive performance-related bonuses or promotions basically have two choices:

1. Disengage by "coasting" (a.k.a., "mentally retiring") until their last day of work

2. Disengage by staying focused and disciplined and leaving a positive legacy

Choice #2 includes mentoring those who will carry on your work, improving work-related processes, nurturing relationships with clients and co-workers (if you have entrepreneurial aspirations, they could hire you for future work projects!), and completing an innovative high profile "legacy project" that will be remembered for years. This is unquestionably the most satisfying and joyful path. In fact, the final years of work could be the most rewarding time in a person's career. Several people told me that training competent "replacements" gave them confidence to leave their employer, knowing that their good work would continue in capable hands.

Conversely, "going through the motions" until departure day (Choice #1) will likely be a boring, sad, and/or stressful process. Nevertheless, researchers have found evidence of preretirement work disengagement. One Dutch study found that position changes via promotions slow down the disengagement process while declining health accelerates it. Bottom line: workers get to choose when and how they disengage.

A key part of the ending phase of transitions is "lasts" (i.e., activities you do or people you see for the last time). If you are leaving a job *and* moving to a new geographic location, there will be even more last-time events to savor (e.g., your last community flea market or holiday concert). The best way to process "lasts" is to recognize them for what they are (e.g., the last time you will likely ever do something again or be somewhere or see a certain person) and document them with photos, videos, and social media.

Moving to the neutral phase of transitions, a key point is that everyone has a different timetable. Mentally switching from decades of working to something new (i.e., Life 2.0) is a gradual progression. Give yourself time to adapt and process the complicated emotions that may be involved (e.g., loss of work identity and a somber realization that you are in the final third of your life). Create a vision of who you want to be and develop a plan to reinvent yourself. Tweak your plans regularly as needed.

Reviewing and revising a "bucket list" written in the past is a good place to start. It can help you identify what you want to experience and why and to let go of aspirations that no longer matter. Select activities (e.g., paid employment and volunteering) purposefully. One study by psychologist Jacquelyn B. James at Boston College found that "only those people who are truly engaged in their post-retirement activities reap the psychological benefits."

Do you still need more direction? In the book *Retire Smart. Retire Happy: Finding Your True Path in Life*, psychologist Nancy Schlossberg identified approaches taken by five different types of people in creating a new life:

- *Continuers*—People who do something similar to what they did in their job, but on their own terms

- *Adventurers*—People who start new activities, learn new skills, and use their time in new ways

- *Searchers*—People who stop and start numerous activities to try out new options through trial and error

- *Easy Gliders*—People who are open to trying almost anything

- *Retreaters*—People who disengage from life and stop doing new things and meeting new people

According to Schlossberg, most people exhibit combinations of several approaches, but one is dominant. Obviously, "retreating" should be avoided because it fosters isolation and poor mental health outcomes.

- **Reflect on Past Transitions**—Think about how you handled major changes previously in your life (e.g., school to work, changing jobs, marriage, divorce, becoming a parent). Identify "learning lessons" from those experiences that can carry over to the transition away from full-time work.

- **Disengage Positively**—Avoid any noticeable decrease in work quality and workplace relationships. Not only will this hurt you if you decide to re-enter the workforce (it will be the last thing that co-workers remember!), but it will not make your final years on the job a pleasant experience.

- **Groom Successors**—Mentor others to carry on your work. Talk them through process steps and share document files. Several people that I interviewed told me they felt they couldn't leave their job because there was nobody qualified to take over. So, they hung on…and on…and on. Develop a legacy project to find competent successors and train them.

- **Let Go on Your Own Terms**—Decide how much of your previous work life, if any, you want to retain and disengage from the rest. For example, you may have belonged to several professional associations before and now decide to belong to only one.

- **Find Your Happy Place**—Do things because you want to, not just because they are expected of you as a parent, grandparent, or former employee. This includes working if you love what you do. Choose activities that provide structure, meaning, and the opportunity to make social connections.

- **Control Your Narrative**—Describe your new identity carefully and deliberately, or others may incorrectly assume that you have disengaged from life, as well as a job. Correct misassumptions when you hear them or see them (e.g., in an e-mail). See Chapter 16 for pointers about describing what you do to others.

- **Get Information Going and Coming**—Review "offboarding" information provided by your former employer (to facilitate disengagement) and "onboarding" information provided by Medicare, Social Security, potential volunteer sites, and other organizations that you will be interacting with.

References

Bagsby, P. (2018). *Four Tips for Keeping Employees Engaged Prior to Retirement.* Q4 Psychological Associates. https://www.q4solutions.com/insights/employees-engaged-retirement/

Bridges, W. (2004). *Transitions: Making Sense of Life's Changes.* Da Capo Lifelong Books.

Chamberlain, J. (2014). *Retiring Minds Want to Know.* American Psychological Association. https://www.apa.org/monitor/2014/01/retiring-minds

Damman, M., Henkens, K., & Kalmijn, M. (2013). Late-Career Work Disengagement: The Role of Proximity to Retirement and Career Experiences. *The Journals of Gerontology Series B*, 68(3), 455-463. https://academic.oup.com/psychsocgerontology/article/68/3/455/559482

4 Must Dos for Making the Transition from Work to Retirement (2016). Leisure Freak. https://www.leisurefreak.com/making-transition-from-work-to-retirement/

Greer. C. (2020). *Tidying Up That Bucket List.* Natural Awakenings. https://www.naturalawakenings.com/2019/12/30/292786/tidying-up-the-bucket-list-deciding-what-we-really-want

Gupta-Sunderji, M. (2018). How to Inspire the Close-to-Retirement Employee. *The Globe and Mail.* https://www.theglobeandmail.com/report-on-business/careers/leadership-lab/how-to-inspire-the-close-to-retirement-employee/article20077647/

Hellmich, N. (2015). Avoid the Shock: How to Ease into Retirement. *USA Today.* https://www.usatoday.com/story/money/2015/01/18/easing-transition-retirement/21815141/

Hester, T. (2016). *Don't Check Out Early: Staying Engaged in the Home Stretch to Early Retirement*. Our Next Life. https://ournextlife.com/2016/10/17/early-checkout/

Lee, K. (2015). 8 Ways to Ease into Retirement. *Everyday Health*. https://www.everydayhealth.com/longevity/future-planning/happy-retirement.aspx

McCalla-Wiggins, B. (2007). *Managing the Transition to Retirement*. NACADA. https://nacada.ksu.edu/Resources/Academic-Advising-Today/View-Articles/Managing-the-Transition-to-Retirement.aspx

Mintzer, D. (2019). Retirement is a Transition, Not a Destination. *Forbes*. https://www.forbes.com/sites/dorianmintzer/2019/01/02/retirement-is-a-transition-not-a-destination/#6ebd759498a1

Schlossberg, N. K. (2003). *Retire Smart, Retire Happy: Finding Your True Path in Life*. American Psychological Association.

What is William Bridges' Transition Model? (n.d.). William Bridges Associates. https://wmbridges.com/what-is-transition/

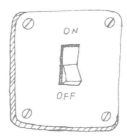

Chapter 25: A New Definition of "Busy"

When people work full-time, about 2,500 hours (50 weeks x 50 hours) or more a year are "spoken for" through work activities and commuting. Many people have lived this way for decades. Demanding jobs, long commutes, household chores, and other "must-do" responsibilities leave little time to loaf. In addition, working is often viewed as a virtue and a sign of value, self-worth, identity, and importance. What happens when you retire, suddenly regain those 2,500 hours, and need to redefine your perception of what it means to be "busy"? For some people, the transition between working and post-work life is almost seamless while others struggle to fill the extra time and figure out what their "new normal" looks like. Feelings of loss, anxiety, disorientation, and disillusionment often follow, but many people are loath to discuss these feelings openly because they are supposedly meant to be "Living the Dream."

Ultimately, individuals are responsible for their own happiness. Retirement literature is rife with stories about new retirees "crashing and burning" after several months of non-working life. Scholars describe a "sugar rush" or "honeymoon period" immediately after leaving work, akin to a long vacation, followed by a decline in happiness months or years later when the novelty of limitless free time wears off. A research paper, "Finding Happiness in Retirement" by Joanna Legutko, concluded that "Financial assets contribute positively to happiness, but retirement happiness is also higher if a retiree is healthy, actively involved with a community, family and friends, and has the option of choosing the time of their retirement as well as the opportunity to derive value in life from work or charitable involvement."

Another study found that the more prestigious and satisfying a person's job was, the more their level of life satisfaction fell after leaving work.

New routines do not just happen—they take time.

Researcher Robert Atchley developed a six-phase model of retirement adjustment that has been widely used as a framework by researchers since the 1970s. Not everyone experiences each phase, but the intention of the model is to provide a general guide to understand gradual financial and emotional adjustments that many people make in later life. The six phases are:

- **Pre-Retirement Planning Time**—Setting goals, saving money, and financial and emotional readiness

- **Retirement Day**—The shortest phase (the final day of work), often marked by celebration and goodbyes

- **Honeymoon Phase**—Savoring newfound "freedom" in a phase that has no set timeframe

- **Disenchantment**—Experiencing a feeling of "letdown," like newly-weds readjusting after a honeymoon

- **Reorientation**—Building a new identity, finding fulfilling activities, and developing new daily routines

- **Routine**—Establishing a new identity, priority activities, daily schedule, and marital time use "rules"

Another way to envision "busy" in later life is to adapt the "Big Rocks" metaphor used by author Dr. Stephen R. Covey. Big rocks (important activities) should be placed in a jar before they get crowded out by gravel (low-priority activities). Gravel can always be poured over rocks later. Part of the reorientation phase in Atchley's model is identifying "Big Rocks" that define "Busy."

If someone continues to work 30 hours per week, for example, that sucks up 1,500 hours per year, leaving only 1,000 hours to fill, plus the continued satisfaction, social interaction, and paycheck that a job provides. Work is a "Big Rock." Similarly, volunteering, daily care of grandchildren (if done joyfully and willingly and not because it is "expected"), social activities with others, and extensive travel are other "Big Rocks." Having much of each day scheduled can help reduce issues that might arise from too much togetherness as described in Chapter 17; spouses can continue to lead partially separate lives when they are apart, as they did for decades before retirement.

Planning (ideally before leaving a job but certainly thereafter) is key to staving off boredom and feelings of uselessness. Talents and skills that took decades to hone can be used in different ways. It is also perfectly fine to kick back, relax, and not jam pack every minute of every day with productivity-based activities. Instead, take time to celebrate just "being." Changing old habits and time-use patterns is a gradual process. After five or more decades of "have to's" (e.g., go to school, get a job, work hard, get promoted), you can now stay busy with "want to's." Give yourself time to figure it out.

- **Schedule Around Your "Big Rocks"**— Identify one or more high-priority activities. If "Big Rocks" take up seven hours a day, sleep takes up eight hours (you have more time!), physical activity takes up one hour, and cooking and eating take up two hours, that leaves six hours of free time— about the same amount that someone has with a full-time job.

- **Keep Working**—Consider finding full-time or part-time work if working is "part of your DNA," is something you enjoy, and/or you need the money. Evaluate your skillset and develop a "pitch" that creates a value proposition for future employers. If you run head-on into the buzz saw of ageism, consider working for yourself as an entrepreneur. Ideally, line up initial clients before transitioning away from a long-time career. Around one in 10 older adults work for themselves.

- **Get a Pet**—Consider adopting a four-legged friend. Animals, especially dogs, can keep people busy, healthy, and happy. They make good companions and help people get exercise, make friends (e.g., meet-ups at dog parks), and feel needed. Some studies have found that people who live with animals are happier and healthier than those who do not.

- **Redefine Productivity**—Be productive on your own terms. When we are working, employers define the productivity metrics that keep people busy through quantifiable means, like billable hours (lawyers), peer-reviewed publications (academics), and number of cars sold (salespeople). In later life, unless you continue working in some capacity, you call the shots. Examples of new productivity metrics include making friends, reading books, and walking steps.

- **Recharge Through Travel**—Consider starting your post-work life with a long bucket-list trip. As an example, long-time AARP financial writer Jane Bryant Quinn announced that she was stepping down in December 2019 and starting her post-work life with a "gap year" living in Rome.

- **Join or Start a Club**—Arrange regular "meetings" with former co-workers over breakfast or lunch, so you stay connected. If you move to an age 55+ community, chances are there will be many established groups to join (e.g., computer club, cooking club, and travel club).

- **Set Five Goals**—Identify five personal and/or professional goals you'd like to pursue with your extra time, then spend most of your time doing activities that support these goals. This process will simplify the number of decisions you need to make. A sample (my five goals for 2020) is shown below.

MY 2020
GOALS

- Stay active in the financial education field via Money Talk work projects, blogging, and social media

- Finish *Flipping a Switch* (my new book) and market it

- Make new friends in Florida and keep in touch with NJ friends and family

- Do lots of fun things and new things

- Stay healthy: Walk 10.000 steps per day, eat healthy foods, get 7+ hours of sleep per night, and keep weight < 122 pounds

References

Call, R. (2019). *What to Do in Retirement: 20 Serious (and Fun!) Things to Keep You Busy.* https://sixtyandme.com/20-serious-and-fun-things-you-can-do-in-retirement/

Chamberlin, J. (2014). *Retiring Minds Want to Know.* American Psychological Association. https://www.apa.org/monitor/2014/01/retiring-minds

Choice 3: Schedule the Big Rocks, Don't Sort the Gravel (n.d.) Franklin Covey. https://www.franklincovey.com/the-5-choices/choice-3.html

Covey, S.R. (n.d.). *The Big Rocks of Life.* http://www.appleseeds.org/Big-Rocks_Covey.htm

Cussen, M.P. (2019). *Journey Through the 6 Stages of Retirement.* Investopedia. https://www.investopedia.com/articles/retirement/07/sixstages.asp

Gay, J. (2018). Working Like Crazy May Actually Be, Well Crazy. *The Wall Street Journal.* https://www.wsj.com/articles/working-like-crazy-may-actually-be-well-crazy-1540570001

Hellmich, N. (2015). Avoid the Shock: How to Ease into Retirement. *USA Today:* https://www.usatoday.com/story/money/2015/01/18/easing-transition-retirement/21815141/

Horner, E.M. (2014). Subjective Well-Being and Retirement: Analysis and Policy Recommendations. *Journal of Happiness Studies*, 15, 125-144. https://link.springer.com/article/10.1007/s10902-012-9399-2

Hughes, D. (2017). 5 Ways Pets Can Add Love to Your Retirement. *U.S. News and World Report:* https://money.usnews.com/money/blogs/

on-retirement/articles/2017-10-12/5-ways-pets-can-add-love-to-your-retirement

Kagan, J. (2018). *Phases of Retirement.* Investopedia. https://www. investopedia.com/terms/p/phases-retirement.asp

Kinsella, C. (2019). *Making a Positive Mental Transition to Retirement.* https://www.heretohelp.bc.ca/making-positive-mental-transition-retirement

Legutko, J. (2014). *Finding Happiness in Retirement.* Actuarial Society of South Africa. https://actuarialsociety.org.za/convention/convention2014/assets/pdf/papers/2014%20ASSA%20Legutko.pdf

Linberg, S. (2019). How to Smoothly Navigate the Identity-Changing Transition into Retirement. *The Week.* https://theweek.com/articles/829190/how-smoothly-navigate-identitychanging-transition-into-retirement

Longhi, S., Nandi, A., Bryan, M, Connolly, S., & Gedikli, C. (2018). *Unhappiness in Unemployment-Is It the Same for Everyone?* Sheffield Economic Research Paper Series, The University of Sheffield. https://pdfs. semanticscholar.org/1066/6f4ba3c05c10450da4a1b72bb727b55a0598.pdf

Loving Life and Staying Busy in Retirement (2020). Nolo.com. https://www. nolo.com/legal-encyclopedia/loving-life-staying-busy-retirement-29597. html

Mitchell, P.A. (2019). *Five Ways to Keep Busy After Retirement.* Aging Options. https://www.agingoptions.com/blog/2019/03/04/five-ways-to-keep-busy-after-retirement/

Morin, A. (2020). *8 Tips for Adjusting to Retirement.* VeryWell Mind. https://www.verywellmind.com/tips-for-adjusting-to-retirement-4173709

Quinn, J.B. (2019). *Jane Bryant Quinn's Parting Retirement Advice.* AARP. https://www.aarp.org/retirement/planning-for-retirement/info-2019/keep-it-simple-strategy.html

Sightings, T. (2019). How to Transition into Retirement. *U.S. News and World Report.* https://money.usnews.com/money/retirement/aging/articles/how-to-transition-into-retirement

10 Exceptional Tips for the Average Joe or Jane as You Transition to Retirement. New Retirement: https://www.newretirement.com/retirement/transition-to-retirement-10-exceptional-tips/

Transitioning into Retirement (2020). RetirementJobs.com. https://retirementjobs.com/career-advice/working-social-security/transitioning-into-retirement/

What to Do in Retirement: How to Keep Busy Using Hobbies, Work, Family, and More (2019). Love and Money. https://www.lovemoney.com/news/62595/what-to-do-in-retirement-ideas-hobbies-work-volunteer-money-happiness

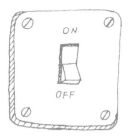

Chapter 26: Increased Interest in Accessibility and Safety

This chapter describes another aging-related switch that flips even though we may not want it to. As people get older, their house, which may have been functional and appropriate for decades, suddenly has challenging "accessibility issues" as a result of disabilities, chronic conditions, arthritis, and more. For example, it becomes difficult to get in and out of a bathtub, navigate changes in flooring (e.g., hard wood floors to carpet), walk up and down stairs, and even grip a doorknob.

The risk of falls increases with age due to diminished eyesight, especially at night and in low light conditions, as well as poor physical strength and balance. The average 60-year-old needs at least three times as much light as the average 20-year-old. Clouded vision (cataracts) can also result in poor vision. Falls are the number one cause of injuries and deaths from injury among older adults. According to a report by the Centers for Disease Control, "Every second of every day in the United States, an older adult falls."

Stated another way, one in four older Americans will fall each year. Two-thirds of those who fall will fall again within six months and more than half of people age 80+ fall annually. The estimated cost to the country (via Medicare) of falls by older Americans in 2014 was a staggering $31 billion. Even more sobering, 25 percent of older adults who break a hip from a fall die within six months, often due to complications from surgery. My mom was one of those statistics.

For the past decade, the National Council on Aging has sponsored Falls Prevention Awareness Day to increase awareness of this growing public health issue. Given the above statistics, making a home accessible and safe takes on an increased urgency in later life. It is important to think seriously about home modifications, safety risks, relocation, and other strategies to live safely and fall-free for the remainder of life. Most people want to remain in their own home, if possible.

Some home modifications are free or inexpensive. For example, removing clutter and throw rugs, buying nonslip mats and rugs, installing grab bars at the entryway and on the back wall of a walk-in shower, rearranging furniture for unobstructed pathways, rearranging pantry closets and kitchen cabinets for easy-to-reach access, and using LED lights and night-lights. In addition, adding peel-and-stick traction strips to floors and stairs, applying nonslip wax on floors, replacing standard toilets with raised toilets, replacing round doorknobs with lever handles and cabinet doorknobs with pull bars, installing automatic garage door openers, and placing a shelf or table by entryways to put packages on while opening the door are other ways to help increase safe accessibility throughout the home.

Other home modifications can be more costly and complex, including converting a conventional bathroom tub into a walk-in tub or shower, installing overhead lights, windows, or skylights to improve natural lighting, installing handrails, widening doorways, installing ramps for a wheelchair, adding a first-floor laundry, investing in "smart home" products (e.g., voice-controlled digital assistants), and installing pull-out drawers. Relocating at least one bedroom and one full bath to the main level of a home or, if this is not possible, adding a home elevator or stair lift are other options.

Aging is a progression. At some point, people may still get around but need assistance with meals or other activities of daily living (ADLs). Two types of housing that require additional "flipped switches" (plus considerable downsizing) are assisted living facilities and continuing care retirement communities (CCRCs). With assisted living, residents typically live in independent units (like an apartment) and pay four- or five-figure monthly fees (depending on location and services provided) for housing and care. With a CCRC, residents typically pay a high six-figure entry fee, plus a monthly fee, for a "continuum of care" ranging from an independent unit to assisted living to skilled nursing care in a nursing home unit, if needed.

HOW TO FLIP THIS SWITCH

- **Remove Safety Hazards**—Pay attention to items that cause falls. Examples include hoses, rugs, pet toys (and, sometimes, even small pets), grandchildren's toys, staircase clutter, electrical extension cords, slick and shiny floors (increases glare), and/or wet, slippery floors, especially in bathrooms.

- **Practice Good Health Habits**—Follow the advice of health experts. Eat a healthy diet, take calcium and vitamin D to keep bones strong, and include weight-bearing activity (e.g., walking) and strength-building exercises in your daily routine. Check out local Silver Sneakers exercise classes for older adults.

- **Improve Flooring**—Install tile and flooring that has a high slip-resistant rating called a coefficient of friction (COF). Retailers can help you select products with COF ratings that comply with Americans with Disabilities Act standards.

- **Improve Lighting**—Do what experts recommend: "layer" light by combining ambient lighting (e.g., normal room lights and natural light from outdoors) with task lighting (e.g., a lamp for reading), and accent lighting (e.g., decorative wall sconce lamps). Make sure hallways are well lit.

- **Renovate with Universal Design**—Choose products that are designed to be functional for people with diverse needs and abilities. Not only will it make your home more comfortable, but it could enhance its resale value, especially if located in an age 55+ community.

- **Consider Multi-Generational Housing**—Consider doubling (or tripling) up. In my small family circle, there are two instances of a 70-something grandparent (my cousin and sister-in-law) living with 40- or 50-something adult children and grandchildren. Family members pool income to cover the mortgage and share care-giving roles.

- **Find Local Resources**—Call 211 or check www.211.org to find out if there are any local or state programs that can assist with home renovation expenses. Some government entities have loans or grants designed to help people stay in their homes.

- **Do Some Math**—Compare the cost of renovating your home versus moving to assisted living or a CCRC. Key questions to ask are: Are you ready for daily assistance with ADLs? How much money will you net from the sale of your house? What is your life expectancy? Can you afford the monthly costs of an assisted living facility (or the entrance fee and monthly fee for a CCRC) without running out of money?

- **Follow the Rule of Three**—Compare at least three assisted living facilities or CCRCs on your own, through referrals, or with the assistance of a senior living specialist. Key factors to consider, besides cost, are proximity to doctors and hospitals, resident activities, cleanliness, and appearance.

References

Aging: What to Expect (2018). Mayo Clinic. https://www.mayoclinic.org/ healthy-lifestyle/healthy-aging/in-depth/aging/art-20046070

Edelman, M. & Ficorelli, C.T. (2012). Keeping Older Adults Safe at Home. *Nursing*, 42(1), 65-66. https://journals.lww.com/nursing/ Fulltext/2012/01000/Keeping_older_adults_safe_at_home.19.aspx

Falls are Leading Cause of Injury and Death in Older Americans (2016). Centers for Disease Control and Prevention. https://www.cdc.gov/media/ releases/2016/p0922-older-adult-falls.html

Glossary of Senior Living Terms (2020). A Place for Mom. https://www. aplaceformom.com/planning-and-advice/articles/glossary-of-senior-living-terms

Herzberg, P. & Boone. L.L. (2017, October). Choosing a Continuing Care Facility. *Journal of Financial Planning*. https://www.onefpa.org/journal/ Pages/OCT17-Choosing-a-Continuing-Care-Facility.aspx

Home Accessibility Checklist (1998). University of Kentucky Extension. http://www2.ca.uky.edu/hes/fcs/factshts/HF-LRA.018.PDF.

Home Modification (n.d.). Live in Place Designs. https://liveinplacedesigns. com/disability-modifications/home-modification-for-elderly-and-disabled/

Home Safety for People with Disabilities (2008). Amputee Coalition of America. https://www.cdss.ca.gov/agedblinddisabled/res/VPTC2/5%20 Injury%20and%20Fall%20Prevention/Home_Safety_for_People_with_ Disabilities.pdf

Jayson, S. (2019). *How to Make a Home Safe for Your Aging Parent.* AARP. https://www.aarp.org/caregiving/home-care/info-2019/safety-tips.html

Keep Older Adults Safe from Injury (2018). Centers for Disease Control and Prevention. https://www.cdc.gov/features/older-adult-safety/index.html

Mercer, K. (2019). *10 Ways to Make a Handicap Accessible Home.* 101 Mobility. https://101mobility.com/blog/10-ways-to-make-a-handicap-accessible-home/

Murray, A. (2018). *A Guide to Helping Senior Citizens Stay Safe at Home.* MyMove. https://www.mymove.com/design/guide-helping-senior-citizens-stay-safe-home-2/

Residential Facilities, Assisted Living, and Nursing Homes (2017). National Institute on Aging. https://www.nia.nih.gov/health/residential-facilities-assisted-living-and-nursing-homes

Silver Sneakers (2020). https://tools.silversneakers.com/

Stringfellow, A. (2019). *Home Modifications for the Elderly.* Seniorlink. https://www.seniorlink.com/blog/home-modifications-for-the-elderly

What is Universal Design? (2020). National Disability Authority. http://universaldesign.ie/What-is-Universal-Design/

What You Need to Know About Assisted Living (2020). WebMD. https://www.webmd.com/healthy-aging/guide/assisted-living#1

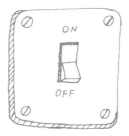

Chapter 27: Should I Stay (Put) or Should I Go?

When someone leaves a job after decades of work, they are technically free to live anywhere. Assuming they have the financial resources to do so (this is another chapter written through a lens of privilege), a question made famous by British rock band The Clash is raised: "Should I Stay or Should I Go?" Some people will ask themselves this question several times during their remaining lifetime. For example, they might consider a move south in their 50s or 60s and a move to assisted living, a CCRC, or to live with a child in their 70s, 80s, or 90s. Research studies and blogs galore describe factors to consider. Ultimately, the decision comes down to weighing pros, cons, and feelings.

According to a survey by the government-backed housing agency, Freddie Mac, almost two-thirds of age 55+ homeowners say they want to "age in place" in their current home. A majority of these homeowners were very satisfied with both their homes and communities. Advantages of staying put include simplicity and less stress (i.e., no need to sell, buy, and move), familiarity (e.g., friends, family, doctors, churches, and community groups), no need to downsize (at least not yet!), and pride of ownership (e.g., prior home improvements and being a "hub" for family visits). Challenges include filling time in between family activities (when you are no longer working) and maintenance and physical challenges associated with an older home.

Conversely, moving hundreds or even thousands of miles from where you previously worked also has advantages: a fresh start, a community of peers and organized social activities (e.g., in age 55+ communities), cost savings (e.g., moving to a state with lower living costs and/or no income taxes), and more desirable weather. However, there are also disadvantages: the effort required to move, make friends, find new professional services and social outlets, and generally just "start over" in a place where, unlike the famed bar on the television show *Cheers,* nobody knows your name. Also underlying the "stay or go?" decision is a desire to have "a good ending" in later life and the fears of ending up alone and vulnerable.

Personal finance writer Jonathan Clements wrote, "When retirees tell me they are moving to a place simply for the warmer weather, low taxes, or affordable housing, I worry that they're making a terrible mistake because they may be miserable without the network of friends they left behind." Conversely, I read stories about people moving away but staying in close contact with family and friends via phone calls, video-chat technology, and social media.

According to an AARP survey, 24 percent of grandparents said they video-chat with their grandchildren at least every couple of weeks. Other writers reported mentally leaving the door open to returning "home" to live with or near family if their spouse died or health deteriorated. Comments like this were common: "Family is more important than anything else, and as you get older, you will need them nearby to help. It is very hard for kids to deal with your aging issues when you are far away." According to one study, the strength of family ties with children determine whether a return move is considered.

Perhaps the best way to decide to make a move (or not) is an old-school matrix with four squares: pros and cons of staying and pros and cons of moving. Read articles about "Best Places to Retire" but note that each defines "best" differently, so pay attention to the metrics they use. The Center for Retirement Research at Boston College notes that, financially speaking, how well people live in retirement depends on their income and the local cost of living. Online cost-of-living calculators provide useful comparisons from one city to another. For example, according to Nerd Wallet's calculator, to maintain a pre-tax income of $100,000 in Morristown, New Jersey one would require $74,876 in Orlando, Florida—about 25 percent less. AARP's Livability Index is another useful resource with scores for communities across the U.S.

- **Do Pre-Move Research**—Visit potential relocation sites during different seasons and follow their local news online via newspaper websites and social media. Consider factors including affordability, amenities, health care quality, safety, weather, potential for natural disasters (e.g., wildfires and hurricanes), and culture (both the arts/entertainment kind and politics).

- **Consider Family Implications**—Think downstream about implications of long-distance moving. When you are no longer able to travel long distances, you are, de facto, requiring your children to spend their money and vacation time to travel to see you (or they will make few visits if they cannot afford it). Also consider the potential for long-distance caregiving in 20 to 30 years, or the possibility of adult children moving you back into their home when you become frail. Most families never discuss these issues at the time of a parent's move.

- **Consider Family Expectations**—Define expectations of "togetherness" if you move to live near a child and determine the role you will play in the lives of children and grandchildren (e.g., the frequency of visits and boundaries for caregiving). Debra Witt wrote in a *Forbes* article, "You want your kids to be honest, so feelings might get hurt. But it's better to have these negotiations before any move because the answer may make you decide not to relocate after all." Also, consider what you might do if a child whom you moved to be closer to has to move, themselves, later on. A neighbor of mine, a "trailing parent," is in this exact situation. She is selling her house solely because her son is moving cross country for a new job.

- **Consider the SALT**—Learn about state and local taxes (SALT) in different parts of the country, especially if you will experience an increase in income with pension benefits and RMD withdrawals. SALT taxes to consider include income, sales, property (real estate and personal property), estate, and inheritance (in Iowa, Kentucky, Maryland, Nebraska, New Jersey, and Pennsylvania) taxes.

- **Build Strong Relationships**—Invest the time required to build social capital with family and friends. Dozens of bloggers concur that aging is difficult without people to help with life's inevitable challenges, and research suggests that "you can't go back home again" without strong family ties. Budget for routine trips back home to reconnect with loved ones. One blogger, Kimberly Blaker, noted in an article for *55 Plus*, "If you live further away, the times you get to spend together will be more focused, special, and memorable."

- **Invest the Time**—Build social connections in your new domicile through volunteering, community organizations, and simply "hanging out" with neighbors. According to retirement happiness experts, people underestimate the difficulty of developing an entirely new social network in later life without the two things that help people make friends at earlier ages: work and children.

- **Weigh the Trade-Offs**—Make a wish list of "must haves" in a later life home. Jonathan Clements listed 10 items, including walking distance to his daughter, a guest bedroom, and a one-story floor plan. Also realize that all choices have trade-offs. For example, moving to a 55+ community could increase expenses but may be well worth it for the built-in social opportunities that it provides.

References

AARP Livability Index (2018). AARP. https://livabilityindex.aarp.org/

Adler, S.E. (2019). *Tech Keeps Grandparents, Grandkids Connected.* AARP. https://www.aarp.org/home-family/personal-technology/info-2019/grandparents-tech-survey.html

Blanton, K. (2020). *Retiree Living Standards, Ranked by State.* Center for Retirement Research at Boston College. https://squaredawayblog.bc.edu/squared-away/retiree-living-standards-ranked-by-state/

Blanton, K. (2020). *Retiring in Florida: The Villages vs. Reality.* Center for Retirement Research at Boston College. https://squaredawayblog.bc.edu/squared-away/retiring-in-florida-the-villages-vs-reality/

Brandon, E. (2014). 7 Reasons Not to Move in Retirement. *U.S. News and World Report.* https://money.usnews.com/money/retirement/articles/2014/01/21/7-reasons-not-to-move-in-retirement

Clements. J. (2020). Rule the Roost. *Humble Dollar Blog.* https://humbledollar.com/2020/02/rule-the-roost/.

Family and Retirement: The Elephant in the Room (2016). Age Wave. http://agewave.com/what-we-do/landmark-research-and-consulting/research-studies/family-retirement-the-elephant-in-the-room/

Fun After Fifty (2016). Freddie Mac. http://www.freddiemac.com/research/insight/20160719_fun_after_fifty.page

Giordano, T. (2018). *Will You Move During Retirement?* Vanguard Blog. https://vanguardblog.com/2019/10/10/will-you-move-during-retirement/

Lloyd, J. (2019). For Boomers Making Plans to Relocate for Retirement, It's Time to Get Real About Risks. *Los Angeles Times.* https://www.latimes.com/business/la-fi-boomer-retirement-moves-20190308-story.html

Moving Away from Family to Better Afford Retirement Living Expenses (2019). After50finances.com. https://www.after50finances.com/retirement-expenses/moving-away-from-family-to-better-afford-retirement/

Moving Away in Retirement (2019). 55 Plus. http://www.roc55.com/features/moving-away-in-retirement/

NerdWallet's Cost of Living Calculator (2020). https://www.nerdwallet.com/cost-of-living-calculator

Price, D. (2017). *Living Where You Love vs. Living Near the Grandkids in Retirement.* Sixty&Me. https://sixtyandme.com/living-where-you-love-vs-living-near-the-grandkids-in-retirement/

Snider, S. (2019). What is Inheritance Tax? *U.S. News and World Report.* https://money.usnews.com/money/personal-finance/taxes/articles/what-is-inheritance-tax

Stoller, E.P. & Longino, C.F. (2001). "Going Home' or "Leaving Home"? The Impact of Person and Place Ties on Anticipated Counterstream Migration. *The Gerontologist*, 1(1), 96-102. https://www.ncbi.nlm.nih.gov/pubmed/11220820

Witt, D. (2019). Should You Move Near Your Grown Child When You Retire? *Forbes.* https://www.forbes.com/sites/nextavenue/2019/08/21/should-you-move-near-your-grown-child-when-you-retire/#5797d6b62e87

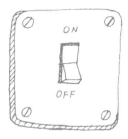

Chapter 28: No More Excuses

After decades of employment, many people have perfected the fine art of using work as an excuse. Phrases like "I wish I could help, but I have to work," "Sorry, I'm swamped with a big work project right now," and "I just don't have the time because I work 60 hours a week with my commute" roll off the tongue easily as a convenient "buffer" against unappealing requests (e.g., volunteering and coaching). For the most part, people accept the "work excuse" because they know that work is necessary to earn money to pay household bills. Certainly, they can't expect you to reduce your work hours and take a pay cut. Like "the cancer card" ("I'm sorry, but I have cancer"), people generally back away and don't press the issue.

A job provides a convenient excuse to "just say no" to many things: healthy eating ("I don't have time to cook"), exercising ("I don't have time to work out"), maintaining relationships ("I am busy working hard to pay my bills"), and moving away from family and friends ("I have to go elsewhere to get a higher-paying position"). A job is blamed for setting your schedule and influencing your decisions. A work excuse is easier for others to accept than if you were to simply say, "I don't have time for you," or "I don't want to live here anymore."

A group of Harvard researchers studied how people react to different excuses given for a hypothetical scenario of going out to dinner with a friend. Three options explored in the study were money used as an excuse ("I don't have enough money"), busyness used as an excuse ("I don't have time"), and no excuse. The study found that people were more sympathetic to money as an excuse versus the other two options because they believed that people "had less personal control over the circumstances they were citing as an excuse." Conversely, time was perceived as a more personally controllable resource than money.

So, what happens when you step away from a job? You lose your go-to excuse. You can no longer blame work for making you do things (or miss things), and you must now own your life decisions. There is no longer a boss, work schedule, or commute to blame for what you do (or don't do). Some people develop new excuses for requests they want to turn down ("I'm busy doing..."), some just say "no" without offering an excuse, and some switch gears and say "yes" to things they have said no to for years (e.g., joining a church committee).

Experts caution that it is just as easy to get over-committed after leaving a job as it was when you were working full-time. Saying "yes" to time-consuming requests too often can result in stress, regret, and resentment. In the Retirement Wisdom blog, retirement coach Joe Casey writes, "One of the surprises new retirees report is that they quickly become much busier than they expected—or wanted—to be. Suddenly, they find themselves as busy as they were before, just with a different mix of activities, but driven too much by other people's priorities rather than theirs. Sort of like work all over again, just without the paycheck."

With former "go-to" work excuses rendered useless, people who are no longer working full time need new phrases to gracefully avoid over-commitment and protect their newly found free time. A perennial favorite is "Thank you for asking me, but I've really got a lot on my plate right now." Some people elaborate further to describe the actual activities or commitments that they are engaged in while others keep their "plate" items a mystery. For all someone knows, it could be something totally self-indulgent like binge-watching a series of television shows. Others do not need to know.

Joe Casey recommends giving a concise reason for "no" responses: "The longer your story, the more likely holes can be punched in it." He also recommends offering names of substitutes to the people who are asking you to do something (e.g., "Have you thought about asking [name]?"), so they can find someone else to do tasks they were hoping you would do.

- **Say No. Period.**—Be firm and say "no" to things you do not want to do—with or without an excuse. Some people find this difficult, however, and hedge their reply with words like "maybe next year" to sound more "polite." The problem with "maybe later" language is that you open the door to another request that needs another response. Instead, politely thank people for asking you and state that you are not interested.

- **Practice Saying Yes**—Develop a new go-to response to replace "Sorry, I have to work." You may be out of practice with saying "yes." Good responses to filter requests to do things without saying yes or no immediately are "I will need some additional information," or "Tell me more." Take time to ask questions and avoid being rushed into a decision. Too many affirmative replies is how people quickly get over-committed.

- **Take Rainchecks**—Follow your gut with respect to limits for taking on additional tasks. There may be times when you really want to say "yes" to opportunities, but the timing is simply not right. Perhaps you have extra caregiving responsibilities right now that are consuming a lot of your time. In this case, state that you will get back in touch when your schedule frees up.

- **Define What You Want**—Refer back to your five personal and/or professional goals for the year, which reflect things that are important in your life and activities that you enjoy doing. Use these goals as "guardrails" for responding to requests to do things. If a requested activity does not support any of your goals, just say no and do not feel guilty about it. Consider saying yes to activities that support your goals.

- **Don't Do Things You'll Regret**—Think about activities that make you happy and those that would likely stress you out. For example, as a financial education entrepreneur, I only say yes to projects that are a good match for my knowledge and skill set and have clearly defined deliverables. I also have to be able to easily estimate a cost and completion time. I say no to any project that requires a lot of background research, a steep technological learning curve, and/or an uncertain time commitment (e.g., online teaching).

- **Reach Out Gingerly**—Remember, after saying "Sorry, but I have to work" for decades, people probably have stopped asking you to do things. You will need to reach out to them if you are interested in pursuing opportunities, but don't expect them to drop everything just because you have more free time. This includes children, grandchildren, friends, and former co-workers. Don't be the person who repeatedly goes back to your former workplace and keeps others from working.

- **Consider Opportunity Costs**—Consider the time use trade-offs of various decisions. Opportunity cost is what you give up when you choose one alternative over another. While opportunity cost is typically used in reference to spending money, it also includes how people spend time. For example, when you turn down certain work projects or full-time babysitting for a grandchild, you preserve time for other things.

References

Braverman, B.(2015). How Saying "No" Can Save Your Retirement. *The Fiscal Times*. http://www.thefiscaltimes.com/2015/06/22/How-Saying-No-Can-Save-Your-Retirement

Buggy, P. (2018). *You Don't *Have* to Do Anything (You Always Have a Choice)*. MindfulAmbition.net. https://mindfulambition.net/own-your-choices/

Casey, J. (2020). *Saying 'No' is a Key Part of the New Retirement Skill Set*. Retirement Wisdom. https://www.retirementwisdom.com/saying-no-is-a-key-part-of-the-new-retirement-skill-set/

Cayer, N. (2018). *Stop Doing What You Don't Like to Do*. Medium.com. https://medium.com/@nicolecayer/this-is-how-to-stop-doing-what-you-dont-like-to-do-a80aa1f85801

Dimingo, N. (2019). *Saying 'I'm Busy' Is a Lame Excuse, So Here's What Harvard Researchers Suggest Successful People Do Instead*. Brobible. https://brobible.com/success/article/work-excuses-im-busy-harvard-research-suggests-successful-people-alternative/

Donnelly, G.E., Wilson, A.V., Whillans, A.V., & Norton, M.I. (2019). *Communicating Resource Scarcity*. Harvard Business School. https://www.hbs.edu/faculty/Publication%20Files/19-066_59e1476c-f83e-4862-9aa7-76551fc56d31.pdf

Hobson, J. (2019). *Here's Why This Author Says You Should Not Retire*. WBUR. https://www.wbur.org/hereandnow/2019/08/06/neil-pasricha-retirement-happiness-equation-work

Mandula, C. (2019). *This First Year of Early Retirement Has Been One of the Hardest of My Life*. MarketWatch. https://www.marketwatch.com/story/

this-first-year-of-early-retirement-has-been-one-of-the-hardest-of-my-life-2018-12-26

Mullen, S. (2017). *Owning Our Choices: We Are Not Entitled to the Lives We Didn't Choose*. Rebelle Society. http://www.rebellesociety.com/2017/03/16/shannonmullen-owning/

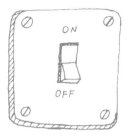

Chapter 29: Pleasing Yourself Instead of Others

For 50 or more years, older adults have been rewarded for being "people pleasers." As children, they were conditioned to please parents and teachers and, as adults, they pleased children, bosses, and clients. "People pleasing" helps us feel valued, avoid guilt, and earn promotions and higher pay. It also reduces judgment by others and affects spending, work habits, and other life decisions.

Once you stop working in a long-term career, consider flipping (or at least dimming) this switch. You can now stop worrying so much about what others want and focus more on pleasing yourself. This is easier said than done, however. After decades of conditioning, the natural response of a "people pleaser" is to meet the needs of and seek validation from others. This often leads to anxiety and resentment over time. The fact is: nobody can please everyone. When people try anyway, they substitute what others want for their own desires and make decisions out of obligation, instead of personal interest, or a fear of doing something that won't be approved of.

Reading dozens of blogs written by and about people-pleasers, a clear take-away is that overcoming people-pleasing tendencies starts with self-awareness; i.e., observing your actions and objectively challenging them with questions like: "Am I doing [activity] because I want to be accepted and others expect it?" and "Will I feel guilty if I don't do [activity]?" If you answer yes, imagine what would happen if you just said no to performing that activity. Like people who leave a job after decades, we often think we are indispensable to others, but people adapt and move on.

Below are some common people-pleasing "switches" shared by my cousin Fran Coletti:

- When do you say enough with dying your hair and let yourself go gray? Do you pencil in your thinning eyebrows until arthritis prevents you from holding the pencil? Do you then have brows tattooed on?

- When do you stop decorating for the holidays?

- When do you pass the wooden spoon and turkey platter to the next generation?

- When do you say "no" to things you've done for the family for years and are "expected"?

Another people-pleasing behavior is acting like a retired person is "supposed to" (i.e., dropping out of the labor force for a life of leisure) when you would personally rather work for income, pleasure, socialization, and/or structure. According to the Employee Benefit Research Institute (EBRI), there is a big disconnect between work plans and reality: 80 percent of workers expect to work for pay in retirement but only 28 percent actually do. Barriers to later life employment include poor health, care-giving, layoffs, and ageism. Nevertheless, over the past 20 years, the share of Americans working in their 70s rose from less than 10 percent to nearly 15 percent.

Some people please themselves and/or try to impress others by denying that they are retired. A study of views about retirement with a sample of 120 retired professionals found interesting insights about how the respondents described themselves. Some put the word "retired" before their former job title (e.g., "retired professor"). Others denied being retired and described their role as if they were still employed (e.g., professor). When asked why, respondents indicated they did not want to be viewed by others as "put out to pasture." One respondent stated, "I don't want to be seen as yesterday's news. I want to be the news right now."

Hundreds of blogs and books warn that the novelty of pure retirement relaxation can quickly wear off, leading to disillusionment and depression. Neil Pasricha, author of *The Happiness Equation*, notes "the two most dangerous years of your life are literally the year you were born and the year you retire." It turns out that, for many people, leaving work, especially when done to please others (e.g., a spouse or child who needs a babysitter), affects three S's for happiness: socialization, structure, and stimulation.

- **Identify People-Pleasing Activities**—Become more self-aware of things you do solely to please others. Make a list of things you think you "have to do" (because people expect them and you have done them for decades). Next, consider whether those activities really have an element of choice. Perhaps some of the "weight" on your shoulders can be lifted through an honest assessment of what you do and why.

- **Decide Who You Will Become**—Think about who you want to be when your formal career ends. This is a prime opportunity to please yourself. If you want to keep working, ideally, have your "next act" ready to launch before your exit. The longer you delay, the harder it will be to market yourself and convince others that you are still relevant. If you plan to focus on volunteer or social activities, explore these new roles.

- **Do Things You Enjoy**—Live consciously by asking yourself some key questions: Am I doing what I want to be doing? Am I happy doing what I am doing? Am I having the impact I want? Am I fulfilled? Blogger Larry Jacobson notes that "fulfillment and purpose are harder to come by than pleasures." He cites this example: "Pleasure is writing an article and seeing it published. Pleasure is fun. Fulfillment is seeing the article you wrote having a positive effect on others. Fulfillment is rewarding."

- **Get in Shape**—Please yourself. Become the best "you" for you with a healthy diet, regular physical activity, and weight loss (if needed). If you have "let yourself go," improved physical appearance is a great self-esteem booster and (right or wrong) enhances employability. Better health can stave off many debilitating conditions. Physical activity has also been associated with a lower risk of cognitive decline in later life.

- **Ditch What You Don't Like**—Live the last third of life on your terms. Work if you want to...or don't. Call yourself "retired"...or don't. Identify people, places, and activities that cause unhappiness and try to stay away from them. Move south if you hate snow and work for yourself if you want flexibility and no commute. Say "no" to things that cause anxiety and resentment and "yes" to things that make you happy. Surround yourself with people who appreciate your authentic self and make you feel supported and empowered.

- **Set Boundaries for Others**—Determine limits of your generosity and communicate them clearly to others. Make it clear through words and actions that you are scaling back on people-pleasing. A colleague's advice for new retirees was "Plan to be caught in the sandwich life-between children's lives and parent's lives." If the sandwich scenario affects you, managing expectations (e.g., sharing of caregiving responsibilities among siblings) and setting boundaries is essential.

- **Anticipate Anxiety**—Let go of things on your own terms: reversing people-pleasing tendencies and communicating new priorities to others may not be easy. Picturing what you want to add to (and eliminate from) your life, establishing new daily routines, and staying socially connected can make the process easier.

- **Embrace Retirement**—Define the "R word" on your own terms. Do fun things and new things. Studies have found that people who view retirement positively (i.e., as a period of growth and opportunity) have better physical and mental health, suffer fewer illnesses, and live longer than those with negative attitudes.

References

Beiber. C. (2019). *80% of Pre-Retirees Think They'll Work in Retirement-Here's How Many Actually Do.* The Motley Fool. https://www.fool.com/retirement/2019/12/15/80-of-pre-retirees-think-theyll-work-in-retirement.aspx

Bishop, R. (2017). *How to Stop Doing Things You Don't Like.* Huffington Post. https://www.huffpost.com/entry/emkeys-to-lifeem-how-to-s_b_124422

Cheng, M. & Kopf, D. (2019). The Number of Americans Working in Their 70s is Skyrocketing. *Quartz.* https://qz.com/work/1632602/the-number-of-americans-working-in-their-70s-is-skyrocketing/

Coletti, F. (2019). Personal Correspondence to the Author.

Coxwell, K. (2019). *Retirement Reinvention: Hold Steady or Become a New You?* NewRetirement. https://www.newretirement.com/retirement/retirement-reinvention/

Hobson, J. (2019). *Here's Why This Author Says You Should Never Retire.* WBUR. https://www.wbur.org/hereandnow/2019/08/06/neil-pasricha-retirement-happiness-equation-work

How to Live Your Best Life in Retirement (2019). Mayo Clinic. https://www.mayoclinic.org/healthy-lifestyle/healthy-aging/in-depth/how-to-live-your-best-life-in-retirement/art-20390076

I Am Now Officially Retiring From 'People Pleasing' (2020). Apost. https://www.apost.com/en/blog/i-am-now-officially-retiring-from-people-pleasing/9968/

Jacobson, L. (2016). The Big Problem New Retirees Run Into. *Forbes.* https://www.forbes.com/sites/nextavenue/2016/06/21/the-big-problem-new-retirees-run-into/#4a127e1575c9

Koulopoulos, T. (2018). It is Time to Say It: Retirement is Dead. This is What Will Take Its Place. *Inc.* https://www.inc.com/thomas-koulopoulos/its-time-to-say-it-retirement-is-dead-this-is-what-will-take-its-place.html

Manning, M. (2016). *4 Things to Do in Retirement If You Want to Find Lasting Happiness.* Sixty and Me. https://sixtyandme.com/4-things-to-do-in-retirement-if-you-want-to-find-lasting-happiness/

Martin, S. (2019). *6 Big Problems with People-Pleasing.* PsychCentral. https://blogs.psychcentral.com/imperfect/2015/11/6-big-problems-with-people-pleasing-and-how-to-fix-them/

Pasricha, N. (2016). *The Happiness Equation.* G.P. Putnam's Sons.

Powell, R. (2016). 6 Ways to Have a Happy Retirement. *USA Today.* https://www.usatoday.com/story/money/columnist/powell/2016/05/25/6-ways-have-happy-retirement/83547956/

Rose, I. (2019). *Why We Lie About Being Retired.* BBC.com. https://www.bbc.com/news/business-48882195

Stansfield, C. (2019). *A Simple Guide to Being Yourself Instead of People Pleasing.* Tiny Budda. https://tinybuddha.com/blog/be-yourself-instead-of-people-pleasing/

Strauss Cohen, I. (2017). No More People Pleasing! *Psychology Today.* https://www.psychologytoday.com/us/blog/your-emotional-meter/201710/no-more-people-pleasing

2019 Retirement Confidence Survey Summary Report (2019). Employee Benefit Research Institute. https://www.ebri.org/docs/default-source/rcs/2019-rcs/2019-rcs-short-report.pdf?sfvrsn=85543f2f_4

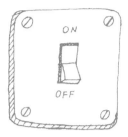

Chapter 30: Seeking Happiness in Later Life

No matter how prepared you think you are, switching to a lifestyle where work is an option, rather than a necessity, is an adjustment. Like becoming a parent, no amount of planning can fully prepare you. Assuming someone has amassed adequate financial resources, a major concern in later life is finding ways to be happy. A century ago, in 1920, average U.S. life expectancy was 53.6 years for men and 54.6 years for women. People often "worked until they dropped." In 2018, average life expectancy was 76.2 for men and 81.2 for women. Older adults, on average, have about 25 "bonus years" to fill. Thoughts like "Okay, now what do I do?" are not uncommon.

At a facilitated "Adjusting to Retirement" discussion group in Ocala, Florida, I heard the following comments:

- "Every week is like having six Saturdays and a Sunday."

- "If you enjoy working, keep on doing it." (Advice from a happy 76-year old worker)

- "Visualize your future; see yourself living elsewhere and doing other things."

- "It is hard to adjust when you don't know what you will do next."

- "Have something planned out, or you will flounder and die early."

- "If you don't have a routine and you have lots of spare time, it leads to bad things."

- "Try to make some advance plans. It can be very stressful to work on your new identity."

- "People who are self-starters have an easier time figuring out what to do."

- "Piece a bunch of activities together and pull back if you get over-committed."

- "You are your own boss. Everything is flexible."

- "Dream a little. Believe in yourself and go for it; this is your time."

- "Assuming your finances are in order, you have options and can give yourself choices."

- "Learn something new every day and read biographies; you can learn a lot from people's stories."

Happiness is an overall sense of well-being where people experience joy and satisfaction. What does research say about later life happiness? Despite many media reports about isolated older adults succumbing to depression, a study by investment firm T. Rowe Price found evidence of optimism. Eight in ten people retired for 11 years or more said they were enjoying their retirement years more than their primary working years, and 86 percent agreed that retirement turned out to be as good or better than expected. Concerns about health care expenses also receded with age. Older retirees were less worried about this than new retirees.

Tau Guo and colleagues studied the relationship between self-reported happiness and daily activities of older adults. Study results indicated that over 6,500 respondents preferred active pursuits like exercising, socializing, and walking, as well as those that require human capital (e.g., volunteering and working) to passive activities, such as staying home and watching television. For retirees in their 60s, the highest level of happiness was achieved when they spent about seven hours a day working or volunteering. For those in their 70s, this time was slightly longer than eight hours, perhaps because they recognized the emotional benefits of social engagement.

The Guo et al. study also found sobering disconnects between how retirees would like to spend their time and what they actually do. While desire for active leisure activities increased with age, so did time spent staying at home and watching television, which led to a decrease in happiness. The researchers noted that active leisure activities often require self-motivation, good health, and financial resources. They may become more difficult to perform over time or awkward to do alone as social networks shrink. Interestingly, the study also found that household wealth was not related to how retirees allocated their time, which, in turn, affected their level of happiness. This finding provides empirical proof that happiness is not something money can buy.

- **Create a Game Plan**—Envision your post-work life before walking away. What will a typical day look like? Decide how you will spend your time and what will make you feel content. For example, you might decide to work and/or volunteer 35 hours per week, which is in line with the Guo et al. study findings. Prioritize activities based on your life goals. Keep a physical or electronic calendar, like you did when you were working, to record daily activities and avoid "double-booking" yourself.

- **Include Your Spouse/Partner**—Discuss activities that you will do alone or with individual friends and things you will do together. Then create an informal schedule based on this discussion. For example, you might devote four days to work, volunteering, or individual pursuits and three days to joint activities. Some older couples even decide to practice a LAT lifestyle—"Living Apart Together"—to accommodate their differing visions of retirement.

- **Set an Exit Date**—Choose the date to leave your long-term career, if you can. Studies have found that people are happier when they leave their job by choice on their own timetable, rather than when retirement is forced on them by layoffs or poor health. To increase the odds of a voluntary exit, invest in your human capital by keeping skills and credentials current.

- **Stay Healthy and Active**—Follow the advice of experts: eat healthy food, exercise regularly, get adequate sleep, reduce stress, and stay socially connected. A study of 3,303 Americans age 25+ by Merrill Lynch and Age Wave found that health care expenses are people's top financial concern in later life and health is viewed as the #1 ingredient for a happy retirement. As the study report notes, "Health can have a far-reaching impact on quality of life, family, and financial security."

- **Learn New Things**—Set a goal to learn one new thing each day and follow the advice of retirement experts to take classes and/or join organizations of people with similar interests. Maintain your skill set and professional certifications to remain current and marketable. Never stop learning.

- **Work on Your "Bucket List"**—Start with the end in mind: your desired lifestyle in retirement. Set goals for which to aim. Make (or update) a list of specific things you want to do and act on it. Don't wait; you are likely not going to be more mobile in later years than you are today. It is magical thinking to assume that your health and abilities in your 80s will be exactly the same as they are in your 60s.

- **Focus on PERMA**—Apply the PERMA model of happiness to your life. According to psychologist Martin Seligman, there are five elements of happiness: **P**ositive emotions, **E**ngagement in activities that bring joy, **R**elationships and social connections, **M**eaning, and **A**chievement.

- **Find Your People**—Focus on activities that make you happy. Go to places you like to be (e.g., gym, community events, clubs, and churches) for opportunities to meet people with similar interests to your own. People are most happy when they can be their authentic selves with others.

- **Practice Gratitude**—Make a mental or written list every day of five things you are grateful for. They do not have to be "big" things like a tax refund but, rather, simple pleasures like an enjoyable cup of coffee or a phone call with a friend. Also remember your personal skill set and advantages that retirement provides: more time for hobbies, exercise, and friends; new experiences; and a more relaxed lifestyle.

- **Monitor Your Finances**—Aim to be debt-free before exiting your career. Retirees without a mortgage or credit card debt have less stress and unhappiness about paying bills or being forced to work to make ends meet. Develop a spending plan to track income and expenses. Include line items for new expenses, such as increased travel and Medigap insurance premiums. If you are worried about the loss of a predictable salary, consider purchasing an immediate annuity that will pay a monthly income for life.

References

Blanton, K. (2020). *Mapping Out a Fulfilling Retirement.* Squared Away Blog. https://squaredawayblog.bc.edu/squared-away/retirement-is-liberating-and-hard-work/

Brandt, A. (2019). 4 Secrets to Finding Purpose and Community After Retirement. *Psychology Today.* https://www.psychologytoday.com/us/blog/mindful-anger/201907/4-secrets-finding-purpose-and-community-after-retirement

Brotman, E. (2019). Changing the Way We View (and Practice) Retirement. *Forbes.* https://www.forbes.com/sites/ericbrotman/2019/01/28/changing-the-way-we-view-and-practice-retirement/#4db0ce949ca4

Brooks, R. (2018). Retired and Loving It? The Differences Between Happy and Unhappy Retirees. *U.S. News and World Report.* https://money.usnews.com/money/retirement/articles/retired-and-loving-it-the-differences-between-happy-and-unhappy-retirees

Buckman, P. (2019). I'm 78 and Refuse to Retire- Here are 9 Things about Happiness and Money We're Often Taught Too Late. *CNBC.* https://www.cnbc.com/2019/09/17/78-year-old-who-refuses-to-retire-shares-important-life-lessons-happiness-success-money.html

Eisenberg, R. (2016). The 9 Keys to a Happy Retirement. *Forbes.* https://www.forbes.com/sites/nextavenue/2016/03/27/the-9-keys-to-a-happy-retirement/#66036b1f40e8

5 Ways to Find Your Purpose in Retirement (2019). Good Life Home Loans. https://goodlifehomeloans.com/finding-your-purpose/

Graham, J. (2018). Older Couples are Increasingly Living Apart. Here's Why. *Time.* https://time.com/5271527/older-couples-living-apart-unmarried/

Guo, T., Cheng, Y., Gibson, P., & Pantuosco, L.J. (2019). Time Allocations and Self-Reported Happiness of Retirees: An Exploratory Study. *Journal of Financial Planning,* 32(3), 38-47. https://www.onefpa.org/journal/Pages/MAR19-Time-Allocations-and-Self-Reported-Happiness-of-Retirees-An-Exploratory-Study.aspx

Health and Retirement: Planning for the Great Unknown (2014). Merrill Lynch. http://agewave.com/wp-content/uploads/2016/07/2014-ML-AW-Health-and-Retirement_Planning-for-the-Great-Unknown.pdf

Johnson, I. (2019). *A Happy Retirement is More Than Just Money.* CNBC. https://www.cnbc.com/2019/03/18/a-happy-retirement-is-more-than-just-money.html

Kristof, K. (2018). Surprise- Money Doesn't Guarantee a Happy Retirement. Here's What Does. *Inc.* https://www.inc.com/magazine/201804/kathy-kristof/happy-retirement-satisfaction-enjoy-life.html

Life Expectancy in the USA, 1900-1998. https://u.demog.berkeley.edu/~andrew/1918/figure2.html

Newman, K. (2020). U.S. Life Expectancy Rises for the First Time in 4 Years. *U.S. News and World Report.* https://www.usnews.com/news/healthiest-communities/articles/2020-01-30/us-life-expectancy-increases-for-first-time-in-4-years

Pagliarini, R. (2019). 3 Strategies That Are Proven to Increase Retirement Happiness. *Forbes.* https://www.forbes.com/sites/

robertpagliarini/2019/02/04/3-strategies-that-are-proven-to-increase-retirement-happiness/#5377e4756695

Pascha, M. (2020). *The PERMA Model: Your Scientific Theory of Happiness.* PositivePsychology.com. https://positivepsychology.com/perma-model/

Powell, R. (2019). *What Makes People Truly Happy in Retirement?* TheStreet.com https://www.thestreet.com/retirement/what-makes-people-truly-happy-in-retirement-14931975

Retirement: Better Than Expected (2020). T. Rowe Price Insights. https://www.troweprice.com/personal-investing/planning-and-research/t-rowe-price-insights/retirement-and-planning/personal-finance/better-than-expected.html

Ruffenbach, G. (2020, February 10). The Definition of a 'Successful" Retirement. *The Wall Street Journal*, R2. https://www.wsj.com/articles/do-you-have-to-be-active-to-have-a-successful-retirement-11581004667

Tergesen, A. (2014). *Will Retirement Pay You a Happiness Bonus?* Market Watch. https://www.marketwatch.com/story/will-retirement-bring-you-a-happiness-bonus-2014-12-17

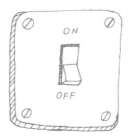

Chapter 31: Green Bananas,
ROLE Calculations, and "Lasts"

Sometime in her mid-70s, my mom started using a strange phrase that felt both perverse and morbid to me: "People my age don't buy green bananas." She used this phrase for over a decade, only partially tongue in cheek, and, as a 40-something, I did not get it. Did she really think that she would die within days before a bunch of green bananas turned yellow and were ripe enough to eat? How could anyone think this way, let alone make that statement over and over to indicate that they thought death was imminent?

But I get it now. As people age, their time orientation changes. It is a "switch" that seems to flip gradually over time. According to researcher Sunghee Lee and colleagues, time orientation is an unconscious cognitive process that provides a framework for organizing personal experiences into temporal categories of past, present, and future. Time orientation is related to important personal traits, such as optimism and sense of control, that affect human behavior. While the green bananas analogy is an extreme example, people do start performing return on life expectancy (ROLE) calculations as they age. In other words, "mental math" comparing how long things might last in relation to their age and life expectancy and whether certain expenses (e.g., an expensive dental crown or a product with a ten-year guarantee) are "worth it."

Time preference researchers use the term "discount rate" to describe the value that people place on future benefits. People with a low discount rate place value on benefits that grow over time (e.g., saving money and healthy behaviors), while those with a high discount rate are not so worried about the future. Older adults tend to have high discount rates and are less concerned about buying things that last decades or saving to buy things. This mindset can drive so-called "senior hedging" decisions, such as buying a used car instead of a new one.

There is, perhaps, no better example of ROLE math calculations than the decision to get a pet in your 60s and beyond. Unlike young adults, who fully expect to outlive one or more pets, older adults often stop to ask what would happen if their pet were to outlive themselves. Average life expectancy for dogs and cats is 10-12 years and 10-14 years, respectively, but there are caveats. Larger dogs (e.g., Great Danes) live for a shorter period of time than smaller dogs (e.g., Chihuahuas), and spaying and neutering a puppy can increase lifespan. Indoor-only cats live longer than those who spend significant unsupervised time outdoors. When pet owners pass away, their pets often end up in an animal shelter, and, unfortunately, many healthy pets that are not adopted are euthanized according to 2nd Chance 4 Pets, a pet rescue advocacy organization.

ROLE calculations can also be applied to big-ticket item purchases: "Will I outlive a new refrigerator?" (average life expectancy: 13 years) or "Will I be around for an extended warranty to be useful after the manufacturer warranty expires?" In addition to weighing the likelihood of an appliance breaking during the extended warranty period and whether a warranty would cost more than a repair, older adults have a layer of ROLE decision-making to consider before they say, "No, I don't need that."

A related concept that affects spending decisions is that of "lasts." Sometimes, at the exact moment that something is happening, we realize it is occurring for the last time in our life. For example, the final time we sit at our desk at a former job—it is a significant moment. Other times, we do not realize a "last" was actually the last time until later. With respect to purchasing decisions, if someone believes a car, house, cruise, or any other big purchase might be the last one of their life, they may decide to spend more lavishly if they have the resources to do so. For example, an average new car in 2020 costs $38,948. However, car costs also include luxury full-size SUVs that average $88,789 and high-performance cars averaging $117,724 with many price points in between. Instead of taking a cruise together, a couple might invite (and pay for) their entire family to join them.

- **Do Some ROLE Calculations**—Think about upcoming major purchases, their average life expectancy according to reputable testing agencies, and whether items you plan to buy can be expected to last the remainder of your lifetime. Consider buying higher quality items than you otherwise might have and properly maintain purchases to increase the odds of having them last longer with fewer repairs.

- **Consider Adopting an Older Pet**—Visit a local animal shelter or pet rescue agency and adopt a dog or cat that is, say, 3 to 5 years old. This way, the pet's remaining life expectancy will be more in sync with its owner's. According to Pet MD, at age 5, dogs that are less than 20 pounds, 20 to 50 pounds, 50 to 90 pounds, and over 90 pounds are equivalent in age to 33, 36, 39, and 42 human years, respectively.

- **Designate a Pet Guardian**—Talk with friends and/or family about your concerns for your pet's future. Find a person to care for your pet if something happens to you (e.g., injury, hospitalization, or death). Also designate a "Plan B" pet guardian in case your first designated pet guardian is unable to step up, or hire a service company, such as PetNet. Make a list of your pet's foods, medical issues, vaccination records, and exercise routines. Designate funds in a will or trust for surrogates to care for your pet.

- **Plan for Emergencies**—Complete the *2ⁿᵈ Chance for Pets Emergency ID Card* that can be downloaded from https://www.2ndchance4pets.org/idcards.pdf and keep it in your wallet. The form includes the pet's name; the pet owner's name, address, and phone number; the veterinarian's name; and the name and phone number of two emergency pet caregivers. It is designed to alert others that there are pets in a person's home to avoid a scenario where pets are left to fend for themselves for an extended period of time in the event of an emergency.

- **Create a Pet Trust**—Consider establishing a trust fund for pets based on their actuarial life expectancy. Identify a primary and contingent trustee, and designate funding for pet care. The trust will also include a residual beneficiary to receive remaining funds, if any, after all pets named as trust beneficiaries pass away.

- **Review Your Resources**—Update your net worth statement and spending plan (budget) annually to see where you stand and consider hiring a financial planner on an hourly basis for periodic financial check-ups. If there is ample evidence that your portfolio is doing well and you will not outlive your assets, consider spending generously on last purchases and last experiences.

References

Average New-Vehicle Prices Up Nearly 2% Year-Over-Year in December 2019, According to Kelley Blue Book (2020). PR Newswire. https://www.prnewswire.com/news-releases/average-new-vehicle-prices-up-nearly-2-year-over-year-in-december-2019-according-to-kelley-blue-book-300980729.html

By the Numbers: How Long Will Your Appliances Last? It Depends. (2009). *Consumer Reports*. https://www.consumerreports.org/cro/news/2009/03/by-the-numbers-how-long-will-your-appliances-last-it-depends/index.htm

Deziel, C. (2017). *How Long Should Appliances Last?* (2017). Landlordology.com. https://www.landlordology.com/long-appliances-last/

Don't Buy the Green Bananas (2007). *Detroit Lakes Tribune*. https://www.dl-online.com/news/530926-pony-express-dont-buy-green-bananas

How Long Do Cats Live? (2020). Pet MD. https://www.petmd.com/blogs/thedailyvet/jcoates/2011/aug/how_long_do_cats_live-11496

How Long Do Dogs Live? (2015). Pet MD. https://www.petmd.com/dog/wellness/evr_dg_how_long_do_dogs_live

How Long Will Your Appliances Last? (2019). *Consumer Reports*. https://www.consumerreports.org/appliances/how-long-will-your-appliances-last/

Huffman, D., Mauer, R., & Mitchell, O.S. (2019). Time Discounting and Economic Decision-Making in the Older Population. *The Journal of the Economics of Ageing*, 14. https://www.sciencedirect.com/science/article/pii/S2212828X16300457

If Anything Happened to You, What Would Happen to Me? (n.d.) 2nd Chance for Pets. https://www.2ndchance4pets.org/ABOUT%202nd%20 Chance%204%20Pets%20July%202019.pdf

Kay, M. F. (2019). Why You Need to Buy Green Bananas. *Forbes.* https:// www.forbes.com/sites/michaelkay/2019/10/01/why-you-need-to-buy-green-bananas/#4306284a6273

Lee, S., Liu, M., & Ho, M. (2017). Relationship Between Future Time Orientation and Item Nonresponse on Subjective Probability Questions: A Cross-Cultural Analysis. *Journal of Cross-Cultural Psychology,* 48(5), 698-717. https://www.ncbi.nlm.nih.gov/pmc/articles/PMC5542685/

Life Expectancy of Dogs and Cats (n.d.). Pet Meds. https:// www.1800petmeds.com/education/life-expectancy-dog-cat-40.htm

Life Expectancy of Dogs: How Long Will My Dog Live? (2018). https://www. caninejournal.com/life-expectancy-of-dogs/

Stettner, M. (2019). *Why Saving-and Spending Money Gets Tricky for Retirees.* MarketWatch. https://www.marketwatch.com/story/why-savingand-spendingmoney-gets-trickier-for-retirees-2019-03-21

The Average Cat Lifespan (2019). https://www.thesprucepets.com/lifespan-of-cats-552035

Vallery, A. (2015). *Planning for What Happens If Your Pet Outlives You.* One Green Planet. https://www.onegreenplanet.org/animalsandnature/planning-for-what-happens-if-your-pet-outlives-you/

What if My Pet Outlives Me? (2016). Daily Press. https://www.dailypress. com/brandpublishing/estate-planning/dp-bp-zaremba-pets-story-story.html

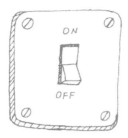

Chapter 32: Self-Regulation and Time-Shifting

Have you ever noticed that when you are very interested in a topic, your "radar" is up to find information about it? It was with me writing this book. Statistics that normally would have gone in one ear and out the other stuck in my brain and germinated to become "flipped switches." At the 2019 New Jersey Foundation for Aging conference, a speaker noted that people in their 60s have the lowest auto accident rates of any decade of life. "Older adults self-regulate," she noted. "They don't drive in snow and heavy rain."

I did some follow-up research and confirmed that drivers age 60 to 69 *are* the safest drivers. According to the AAA Foundation, they have the fewest crashes, injury crashes, and fatal crashes per 100 million miles driven in relation to driver age. Not surprisingly, drivers in their teens have the highest number of crashes and injury crashes and are second in fatal crashes. Drivers age 80+ are number one for fatal crashes, which is attributed to underlying medical conditions and age-related vulnerabilities (e.g., fragile bones) that hinder accident recovery.

According to the Rand Corporation, by 2025, drivers age 65 and older will comprise 25 percent of the driving population versus 15 percent in 2001. Compared to other age groups, older drivers have more driving experience and are more likely to wear seat belts, observe speed limits, and not drink (or be distracted by texting) while driving. Older drivers also journey shorter distances and with less frequency than younger drivers, and, as noted above, they "self-regulate" to avoid driving conditions that put them at risk or to compensate for physical declines, such as vision impairment, slower reaction time, and reduced spatial judgment.

Less driving confidence was also found by researchers to be a trigger for older self-regulated drivers. Older drivers' self-perception of their driving ability directly influences decisions to self-regulate. Studies have found evidence of two different types of self-regulation with respect to driving by older adults:

- *Strategic Self-Regulation* (e.g., not driving alone, at night, on freeways, at rush hour, and in bad weather)

- *Tactical Self-Regulation* (e.g., not chatting with passengers, leaving more distance between a car ahead, and avoiding in-vehicle distractions, such as eating, talking on a cell phone, and changing the radio station)

Strategic self-regulation encompasses decisions that people make before they actually start driving, including the decision to stay home. Tactical self-regulation occurs when drivers are already out on the road.

By definition, a self-regulator's world gradually gets smaller. It is a very difficult switch to flip. In addition to not driving in bad weather, many older drivers quit driving at night and avoid late afternoon trips where they will come home in the dark. They may also decide to stay off roads during peak times (e.g., rush hour) and avoid certain types of roads (e.g., interstate highways). Eventually, driving is confined to a short radius from home or older drivers stop driving entirely, often at the insistence of concerned family members who worry that they are a risk to themselves and other drivers.

I saw self-regulation firsthand during a visit with a former mentor, now in her 90s, who told me that she only drives during daylight in good weather on low-traffic roads close to home. She clearly self-regulates her driving to a point where she feels safe and comfortable. My mom gradually did the same and also announced in her late 70s that she would never fly on an airplane again. She never did.

Closely associated with self-regulation is the concept of "time-shifting"; i.e., switching activities from one time period to another as self-regulating drivers often do. When people are free from the constraints of a full-time job, they are able to time-shift many activities, including banking, eating out, food shopping, and travel, to times when everyone else is working (a.k.a., off-peaking). Doing things at off-peak days and times is less stressful and often results in saving money and having a better experience (e.g., less traffic, fewer crowds, shorter lines).

There is perhaps no better way to experience time-shifting than leisure travel. For example, visiting a busy national park on a weekday in the fall rather than during the summer when families with children are there in droves. Off-peak travelers also have the ability to snag good deals on airfare. Years ago, Tuesday afternoons were considered the best time to book flights because many airlines released weekly airfare sales on Tuesdays. Sundays, more than 21 days in advance of a trip, are now the recommended time for ticket-buying. The cheapest departure days to fly for low fares are Thursday and Friday. Off-peaking can save you hundreds, or even thousands, of dollars on airfare, cruises, admission fees, and hotels.

- **Don't Procrastinate**—Start ticking "to do" items off of your "bucket list." It will not get easier to drive long distances or travel through airports as you get older. According to Michael Stein, author of *The Prosperous Retirememt*, there are three stages of retirement: go-go, slow-go, and no-go. The go-go years right after leaving a job are the most active stage and likely the time when most travel will take place. If you keep putting things off, health issues, widowhood, or death may preclude them ever from happening at all.

- **Self-Regulate as Needed**—Anticipate the potential loss of visual, cognitive, and/or motor skills as you age. These changes will likely affect your confidence level and abilities with respect to physical activity, travel, and other endeavors. Go with your gut with respect to self-regulating personal behaviors for your safety and the safety of others. Practice both strategic and tactical self-regulation.

- **Take a Driver Improvement Course**—Contact your local AAA office for information about "mature operator" courses designed for drivers age 55 and older. Driver education courses may be available online or in a classroom and contain information about defensive driving techniques and the latest vehicle technologies, such as lane-departure warning systems, back-up cameras, and adaptive cruise control that automatically adjusts vehicle speed to maintain a safe distance back from other cars. Not only will these courses teach you important driving skills, but they could also reduce your auto insurance premium.

- **Identify Transportation Services**—Develop a plan for getting around if you start self-regulating your driving or decide not to drive at all. Do research on alternative transportation options before a crisis occurs. For example, family caregivers, government and non-profit agency transportation services, public transit (e.g., busses), airport shuttle services, taxis, and on-demand driving services, such as Lyft and Uber. Allocate more money in your household budget to pay for new transportation expenses.

- **Become a Time-Shifter**—Identify errands and activities that can be time-shifted (from when you did them previously) to save time and money. Experiment with different routines with an eye toward doing things when everybody else is busy. Avoid food shopping on weekends, for example, or lunchtime crowds at your favorite restaurant. Arrive at 11:45 am to avoid parking hassles and waiting for a table.

- **Travel at Off-Peak Times**—Search online for travel deals and consider traveling during the less expensive "shoulder season" right before and after high-cost peak season dates. Also, be flexible with travel dates, especially around holidays. Leave earlier and come home later than other travelers when you no longer have to get home immediately to work.

References

Adcock, S. (2015). *Make Life Awesome by Living Off Peak.* ThinkSaveRetire. https://thinksaveretire.com/make-life-awesome-by-living-off-peak/.

Background On: Older Drivers (2019). Insurance Information Institute. https://www.iii.org/article/background-on-older-drivers

Carmel, S., Rechavi, T.B., & Ben-Moshe, Y. (2013). *Antecedents of Self-Regulation in driving Among Older Drivers.* Cambridge Care. https://www.cambridge.org/core/journals/ageing-and-society/article/antecedents-of-selfregulation-in-driving-among-older-drivers/71F088EDBE05A76E91A1C B37E006AB4F

Cutolo, M. (2018). The Best Time to Book Your Plane Tickets is No Longer on a Tuesday (2018). *Reader's Digest.* https://www.businessinsider.com/the-best-time-to-book-your-plane-tickets-is-no-longer-on-a-tuesday-2018-5

Cutolo, M. (2020). The Best Day to Buy Airline Tickets. *Reader's Digest.* https://www.rd.com/advice/travel/when-to-buy-plane-tickets/

Driver Improvement Courses for Seniors (2020). AAA. https://seniordriving. aaa.com/maintain-mobility-independence/driver-improvement-courses-seniors/

Loughran, D.S., Seabury, S.A., & Zakaras, L. (2007). *What Risks Do Older Drivers Pose to Traffic Safety?* Rand Corporation. https://www.rand.org/pubs/ research_briefs/RB9272.html

Molnar, L.J.(2015). *Self-Regulation of Driving by Older Adults: What Do We Know?* University of Michigan Transportation Research Institute. https:// www.michigan.gov/documents/msp/Strategies_and_Resources_for_Aging_ Drivers-Molnar_485685_7.pdf

Molnar, L.J., Charlton, J.L., Eby, D.W., Langford, J. Koppel, S., Kolenic, G.E., & Marshall, S. (2014). Factors Affecting Self-Regulatory Driving Practices Among Older Adults. *Traffic Injury Prevention,* 15(3), 262-272. https://www.ncbi.nlm.nih.gov/pubmed/24372498.

Rates of Motor Vehicle Crashes, Injuries and Death in Relation to Driver Age, United States, 2014-2015 (2017). AAA Foundation. https://aaafoundation. org/rates-motor-vehicle-crashes-injuries-deaths-relation-driver-age-united-states-2014-2015/

Self-Regulation of Driving by Older Adults: A LongROAD Study (2015). AAA Foundation for Traffic Safety. https://aaafoundation.org/self-regulation-driving-older-adults/

Self-Regulation of Older Drivers (2017). Clearinghouse for Older Road User Safety. https://www.roadsafeseniors.org/blog/self-regulation-older-drivers

Senior Driving (2020). AAA. https://seniordriving.aaa.com/resources-family-friends/conversations-about-driving/facts-research/

Stein, M. (1998). *The Prosperous Retirement.* Emstco Press.

7 Ways to Make Errands Less Stressful (2020). *Reader's Digest.* https://www. readersdigest.ca/health/relationships/7-ways-make-errands-less-stressful-0/

Taylor, D. (2014). *Life Stages in Retirement.* Bankrate. https://www.bankrate. com/financing/senior-living/life-stages-in-retirement/

Timmermann, T. (2019). *The Best Day and Time to Book a Cheap Flight.* Clark.com. https://clark.com/travel/best-day-book-cheap-flight/

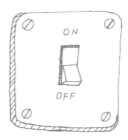

Chapter 33: Invincible to Vulnerable

Like ROLE calculations and self-regulation, sometime in later life it hits you that you are not "invincible" any longer. You have health "issues" (or will have them) and, instead, are vulnerable. There was no better reminder of this than the COVID-19 (Coronavirus) health scare. Suddenly, government officials referred to everyone over age 65 (and, in some cases, even younger!) as "the elderly" and "high risk." Even more sobering, at one point in early 2020, five "elderly" septuagenarians were vying for the office of president of the United States.

For a 60-something who doesn't view myself as "elderly," I was in serious denial about my personal COVID-19 risk until I read the rationale underlying the Centers for Disease Control and Prevention's (CDC) messaging: older adults were about twice as likely as others to develop complications from COVID-19. Two explanations provided were a gradual deterioration of the immune system, making it harder to fight diseases and infection, and increased likelihood of underlying conditions (e.g., heart disease, cancer, and diabetes) that hinder recovery from illnesses. Suddenly, the special "senior hour" at supermarkets for older adults made sense as a way to reduce older adults' exposure to large crowds. According to the National Council on Aging (NCOA), about 92 percent of older adults have at least one chronic disease and 77 percent have at least two. Not surprisingly, older adults have about twice the number of annual visits to physicians as those aged 45 to 64.

Before describing health care challenges of older adults, it is important to note that "the elderly" can encompass people 35 or more years apart in age from 65 to 100+. Therefore, all older adults should not simply be lumped together. Health care researchers and practitioners often use three subcategories of older adults developed by psychologist Bernice Neugarten—"young old" (ages 65 to 74), "old" (ages 74 to 84), and "old old" (ages 85+)—for a more accurate understanding of changes in health status. The "old old" age group is the fastest growing age demographic in the United States. Not surprisingly, aging—as well as family health history, environment, and lifestyle—are key risk factors for various medical conditions.

A key focus of health care in later life is prevention, i.e., staving off disease and injury as long as possible. Our lives and quality of life depend on it. Some of the most common health care challenges of older adults include arthritis, heart disease, stroke, cancer, respiratory diseases (e.g., chronic pulmonary disease and asthma), dementia (including Alzheimer's disease), diabetes, mental disorders (e.g., depression), HIV/AIDS and other sexually transmitted diseases, osteoporosis, and bladder control. Heart disease is the leading killer of adults over age 65, and age is the biggest risk factor for developing cancer. Also, as people age, they increasingly develop and live with two key risk factors for heart disease or a stroke: high cholesterol and high blood pressure. They are also vulnerable when they experience influenza and pneumonia as a result of weakened immune systems.

Another health care challenge is falls, which are the leading cause of injury to older adults. Every 15 seconds, an older adult is admitted to an emergency room for a fall, and, every 29 minutes, a fall injury results in death. About a quarter of adults age 65 and older fall each year, but less than half tell their doctors. About 20 to 30 percent suffer moderate to severe injuries (e.g., hip fractures). One reason for falls is shrinking bones and muscle mass, which makes older adults susceptible to loss of balance, resulting in falls and fractures. In addition, osteoporosis and osteoarthritis contribute to bone frailty, and joints become inflamed and painful.

One or more sensory impairments (sight, hearing, taste, smell, and spatial awareness) are also common in later life. According to the CDC, one in four older adults has a hearing impairment and one in six has a visual impairment (e.g., macular degeneration, cataracts, and glaucoma). Oral health is another health care challenge, especially since many people lose access to dental insurance after they retire. About 25 percent of adults over age 65 no longer have their natural teeth. Another health care challenge is shingles, which affects one of every three Americans age 60 and over, half of those under age 80.

- **Accept Your Vulnerability**—Remember, even if "65 is the new 45," you still have a body that is more than six decades old. Even if you feel your health is very good or excellent as 41 percent of people over 65 did according to a CDC survey, you cannot stop the aging process. Your immune system, stamina, muscle mass, balance, and other physical characteristics are not what they once were. Period. Relinquish the "cloak of invincibility" and heed the advice of experts who describe people your age (or younger) as "high risk."

- **Stave Off and Delay**—Do all you can to avoid injury (e.g., falls) and push back the start of age-related chronic diseases, such as diabetes. Benefits include a higher quality of life for a longer period of time and fewer wealth-draining medical expenses. According to the American Diabetes Association, people with diabetes spend $16,752 a year on medical expenses with $9,601 attributable to diabetes. Postponing diabetes by 10 years can save someone almost $100,000 over that time! Learn the risk factors for various diseases and heed them. Also explore your family health history and share information with your doctor, so it can be acted upon.

- **Avoid Hospitalization**—Understand statistics working against you as motivation to avoid a hospital stay. As the COVID-19 experience indicated, the health care system's capacity has its limits. Even without a global pandemic, there are approximately 74 million living Baby Boomers who will be competing for health care services as they did for classrooms in the 1950s and jobs in the 1970s. A shortage of doctors, especially geriatricians, nurses, and other health care personnel will further compound health care service delivery problems. Expect to use more telemedicine technology, physician assistants, and medication management apps in future years.

- **Follow Healthy Lifestyle Recommendations**—Eat "nutrient dense" foods that provide essential nutrients without empty calories. Examples include fruits and vegetables, whole grains, and lean meats. Cut out sugar-sweetened beverages. Regular physical activity (at least 150 minutes per week of moderate-intensity aerobic activity, such as brisk walking or swimming) and a healthy weight (body mass index or BMI under 25) can also help avoid health problems. Search "BMI Calculator" online to determine your BMI based on height and weight. To lower your risk of cancer, lung disease, and poor surgical recovery, do not smoke.

- **Get Recommended Vaccines**—Follow CDC recommendations for older adults: a flu shot every year and a tetanus booster every 10 years. Also, two doses of Shingrix, the shingles vaccine, starting at age 50 with doses separated by two to six months. In addition, two pneumonia vaccines, spaced one year apart, for everyone age 65 and older are recommended. The first vaccine is PCV13 (Prevnar 13™) followed by PPSV23 (Pneumovax™ 23).

- **Get Recommended Screening Tests**—Get recommended screening tests to ward off diseases or identify and treat them early. Commonly recommended tests for older adults include a blood pressure check at least annually and periodic tests for cholesterol, type 2 diabetes, and bone density. In addition, breast, cervical, colorectal, and prostate cancer screening tests at a frequency determined in consultation with your doctor. Also see a dentist at least annually for a check up and brush and floss your teeth at least twice daily.

References

About Adult BMI (2017). Centers for Disease Control and Prevention. https://www.cdc.gov/healthyweight/assessing/bmi/adult_bmi/index. html#Definition

Bailey, S. (2019). Technology: Health Care Solve for Elders? *Today's Geriatric Medicine.* https://www.todaysgeriatricmedicine.com/news/ex_091415.shtml

Bennett, J.A. & Flaherty-Robb, M.K. (2003). Issues Affecting the Health of Older Citizens: Meeting the Challenge. *The Online Journal of Issues in Nursing,* 8(2). https://ojin.nursingworld.org/MainMenuCategories/ ANAMarketplace/ANAPeriodicals/OJIN/TableofContents/Volume82003/ No2May2003/OlderCitizensHealthIssues.html

Cameron, K. (2020). *Coronavirus: What Older Adults Need to Know.* National Council on Aging (NCOA). https://www.ncoa.org/blog/ coronavirus-what-older-adults-need-to-know/

Chotiner, I. (2020). How Old is Too Old to Work?. *The New Yorker.* https:// www.newyorker.com/news/q-and-a/how-old-is-too-old-to-work

Fry, R. (2018). *Millennials Projected to Overtake Baby Boomers as America's Largest Generation.* Pew Research Center. https://www.pewresearch.org/fact-tank/2018/03/01/millennials-overtake-baby-boomers/

Healthy Aging (NN). Medline Plus. https://medlineplus.gov/healthyaging. html

Move Your Way (n.d.). U.S. Department of Health and Human Services. https://health.gov/sites/default/files/2019-11/PAG_MYW_OlderAdult_ Poster.pdf

Nabili, S. & Davis, C.P. (2020). *Senior Health: Successful Aging.* MedicineNet. https://www.medicinenet.com/senior_health/article. htm#what_are_some_common_facts_about_health_in_seniors

Nania, R. (2020). *Coronavirus and Older Adults: Your Questions Answered.* AARP. https://www.aarp.org/health/conditions-treatments/info-2020/cdc-covid-19.html

Older Adults (2020). HealthyPeople.gov. https://www.healthypeople.gov/2020/topics-objectives/topic/older-adults

People at Risk for Serious Illness from COVID-19 (2020). Centers for Disease Control and Prevention. https://www.cdc.gov/coronavirus/2019-ncov/specific-groups/high-risk-complications.html

Preventive Care for Seniors (2019). Family Doctor.org. https://familydoctor.org/preventative-care-seniors/

QuickStats: Percentage of Adults Aged ≥65 Years Who Reported Excellent or Very Good Health (2013). Centers for Disease Control and Prevention. https://www.cdc.gov/mmwr/preview/mmwrhtml/mm6221a5.htm

Roberts, C. (2018). Health Checklist for Seniors. *Consumer Reports.* https://www.consumerreports.org/seniors-health/health-checklist-for-seniors/

Sensory Impairment and Health Expectancy in Older Adults (2019). Duke Medical School. https://www.sciencedaily.com/releases/2019/08/190815093101.htm

Shrivastava, S., Shrivastava, P. & Ramasamy, J. (2013). Health-Care of Elderly: Determinants, Needs and Services. *International Journal of Preventive Medicine,* 4(10), 1224-1225. https://www.ncbi.nlm.nih.gov/pmc/articles/PMC3843313/

6 Special Healthcare Needs of Seniors (2018). Pasadena Health Center. https://www.pasadenahealthcenter.com/2018/06/08/6-special-healthcare-needs-seniors/

10 Common Elderly Health Issues (2016). Vital Record. https://vitalrecord.tamhsc.edu/10-common-elderly-health-issues/

The Cost of Diabetes. American Diabetes Association. https://www.diabetes.org/resources/statistics/cost-diabetes

The Top 10 Health Concerns for Seniors (2017). American Senior Communities. https://www.asccare.com/health-concerns-for-seniors/

Vann, M. R. The 15 Most Common Health Concerns for Seniors (2016). *Everyday Health.* https://www.everydayhealth.com/news/most-common-health-concerns-seniors/

What is Sensory Impairment? (2020). Reading.gov.UK. http://servicesguide.reading.gov.uk/kb5/reading/directory/advice.page?id=yjdblhTe_x0

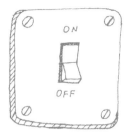

Chapter 34: Handling Wild Card Events

A "wild card' is something unknown and unpredictable. For example, political pollsters often talk about certain issues or demographic groups as being "wild cards" in an election because they are unsure if votes will be affected. Since wild cards are uncertain, people never know in advance if specific wild card events will affect them personally and, if so, when they will occur. For example, if you predecease your spouse while being of sound mind, you will never be a widow or person with dementia. This chapter describes three common later life wild card "switches": widowhood, gray divorce, and diminished capacity. Not every older adult will experience each wild card event but, if they do, the result can be severe emotional and financial stress.

Widowhood

Few events can turn a person's life upside down as much as the death of a spouse, especially if it is sudden and unexpected. In addition to grief associated with death and the loss of a spouse's emotional support and companionship, there is often less household income for the surviving spouse than before. Meanwhile, many household bills stay the same or increase if there are high medical or funeral expenses. In addition, there are many decisions that need to be made (e.g., investing proceeds of a life insurance policy), forms to be completed (e.g., pensions, Social Security), and suggestions from "helpful" family members and/or financial advisors. For some widows and widowers, the pressure to do something—anything—becomes unbearable. Thinking is muddled and decisions may be made quickly, like a "hot potato" that must quickly be tossed away.

According to the U.S. Census Bureau, the average age of onset of widowhood is 59 and widows are likely to live another two decades or more on their own. Widows outnumber widowers by a factor of four, and 70 percent of all married women will experience widowhood at least once during their lifetime. Among people age 75 and older, nearly 25 percent of men and 66 percent of women are widowed. Financial advisor Kathleen Rehl describes three stages of widowhood: grief (i.e., focusing day by day), growth (i.e., starting to plan ahead), and grace (i.e., living a redesigned life). Research by Merrill Lynch in partnership with Age Wave found that the hardest financial challenge in widowhood is becoming the sole decision maker (69 percent), followed by adjusting to a loss in income (67 percent), and navigating financial and legal paperwork (66 percent).

Gray Divorce

Recent cohorts of older adults are divorcing at unprecedented levels. Roughly one-third of marriage dissolutions among couples age 50 and older occur though divorce rather than widowhood, and the divorce rate has roughly doubled since the 1990s. Divorce is stressful for many people who are expected to make rational and far-reaching decisions at a time of emotional turmoil. This may also be their first experience with the court system and expenses often increase when spouses set up separate households. So-called "gray divorces" (a.k.a., "silver splits") between older adults married for decades are especially challenging because they come on the cusp of (or during) retirement when it is difficult to replenish lost assets or generate additional income. There is also often a need to downsize and concerns about health care and a division of retirement savings-plan benefits.

Over a third (34 percent) of gray divorces occur among couples married longer than 30 years, and 12 percent among those married longer than 40 years. While still sitting at half the divorce rate of couples under age 50, gray divorce rates have risen much more dramatically. Common causes of gray divorces cited in research studies and blogs include: increased life expectancy, couples growing apart, spouses expecting greater happiness or feeling entitled to live life more fully, the reduced stigma of divorce, both spouses working and becoming financially independent, the loss of "buffers" such as busy careers and raising children, and different ideas about what retirement should look like. In general, spouses who initiate gray divorces have an easier time coping than spouses who do not because they have been planning in advance about when and how to leave.

Diminished Capacity

Cognitive capacity often declines with age. About half of Americans are expected to develop dementia in their lifetime. Projections are that the most common cause of dementia, Alzheimer's disease, could potentially affect 8 million people by 2030, up from 5 million in 2013. With cognitive impairment comes diminished capacity to understand and retain information, use information to make decisions, and communicate decisions to others.

One of the first signs of diminished capacity is problems managing finances. Even routine financial activities (cash transactions, bank statement management, and bill payment) become difficult, making impaired individuals ripe for exploitation and loss of wealth that took decades to amass. With 50/50 odds of losing the ability to manage finances, the phrase "Hope for the best, but plan for the worst" is appropriate. People often think they will "catch themselves in time" but then dismiss signs of dementia as innocent signs of aging.

Widowhood

- **Take Your Time**—Do not make major financial decisions immediately. If you receive an insurance settlement or other payment, place it in a money market fund or CD until you have time to explore longer-term investment alternatives. Financial planner and author Susan Bradley coined the term Decision Free Zone® (DFZ) to indicate a time for widowed spouses to make only decisions that must be made.

- **Secure Resources**—Contact your spouse's former employer about spousal health and/or pension benefits. Other resources include the face value of life insurance policies and the deceased's retirement accounts (e.g., IRAs and 401(k)s) and veteran's benefits (e.g., burial in a national cemetery).

- **Revise Documents**—Retitle the deceased spouse's or jointly held assets in the survivor's name and review and, if necessary, revise the surviving spouse's will and primary and contingent beneficiary designations.

- **Seek Professional Advice**—Consider hiring an attorney to prepare estate tax returns or a certified financial planner® for investment questions. Ask questions about anything that you do not understand or feel comfortable with. There are no "dumb" questions when your future financial security is at stake.

Gray Divorce

- **Mediate Instead of Litigate**—Consider hiring a professional mediator to reduce the legal costs, time, and stress associated with a divorce that is negotiated by lawyers. Mediators are trained to not "take sides," but, rather, to work out a settlement that is fair and equitable for both spouses. Once issues are resolved, each spouse's attorney can assist with a final agreement.

- **Swap Assets Carefully**—Recognize that 50/50 splits of assets are not necessarily equal. For example, spouses who keep capital assets have embedded capital gains (e.g., stock) or ongoing expenses (e.g., houses). In gray divorces, the division of retirement savings plans and pensions is especially important.

- **Consider Social Security**—Apply for benefits in an ex-spouse's name if they are higher than yours. To qualify for benefits, the marriage must have lasted 10 years and both ex-spouses must be at least age 62.

Diminished Capacity

- **Prepare Legal Documents**—Get the following estate planning documents in place before the onset of cognitive impairments: durable power of attorney, will, living will (advance directive), health care power of attorney (proxy), and (especially with considerable wealth or a family history of dementia) living trust.

- **Designate Trusted Contacts**—Provide financial advisors and financial institutions with the name of a trusted person to contact if unusual account activity or fraud is suspected.

- **Consider Hiring Support Services**—Contact the American Association of Daily Money Managers for assistance with basic financial transactions, if needed.

References

Adams, S.D. & Lichtenburg, P.A. (2014). How to Protect and Help Clients with Diminished Capacity. The *Journal of Financial Planning.* https://www.onefpa.org/journal/Pages/APR14-How-to-Protect-and-Help-Clients-with-Diminished-Capacity.aspx

Bradley, S. (2018). *On Widows and Decision Free Zones.* Financial Transitionist Institute. https://financialtransitionist.com/widows-and-decision-free-zones/

Bradley, S. & Martin, M. (2000). *Sudden Money: Managing a Financial Windfall.* Wiley. https://www.amazon.com/Sudden-Money-Managing-Financial-Windfall/dp/0471380865

Brown, S.L. & Lin, I. (2019). 'Til Death Do Us Part? Declining Widowhood and Rising Gray Divorce, 1980-2017. *Innovation in Aging,* 3(1), S805-S806. https://www.ncbi.nlm.nih.gov/pmc/articles/PMC6845024/

Cahn, N. (2017). *Who is at Risk for a Gray Divorce? It Depends.* Institute for Family Studies. https://ifstudies.org/blog/who-is-at-risk-for-a-gray-divorce-it-depends

Carr, D. (2015). Marital Transitions: Widowhood, Divorce, and Remarriage. *The Encyclopedia of Adulthood and Aging.* https://onlinelibrary.wiley.com/doi/abs/10.1002/9781118521373.wbeaa289

Cheng, M. (2019). Grey Divorce: Its Reasons and Its Implications. *Forbes.* https://www.forbes.com/sites/margueritacheng/2019/02/26/grey-divorce-its-reasons-its-implications/#468f393f4acd

Colson, B. (2020). *Gray Divorce: The Complete Guide.* Survive Divorce. https://www.survivedivorce.com/gray-divorce

Dillon, J. (VV). *Facing a Gray Divorce? Watch Out for These 7 Critical Issues.* Equitable Mediation. https://www.equitablemediation.com/blog/gray-divorce

Fontinelle, A. (2019). *Preparing for Diminished Mental Capacity as You Age.* Mass Mutual Blog. https://blog.massmutual.com/post/diminished-capacity-prepare

Franklin, M. (2019). Dealing with Widows Requires Empathy and Patience. *Investment News.* https://www.investmentnews.com/dealing-with-widows-requires-empathy-and-patience-79649

Godfrey, N. (2019). The Rise of Gray Divorce: Why and Why Not? *Kiplinger.* https://www.kiplinger.com/article/retirement/T065-C032-S014-the-rise-of-gray-divorce-why-and-why-not.html

Kwok, R. & Kern, D. (2017). Cognitive Decline: The Importance of Awareness and Advance Planning. *Journal of Financial Planning.* https://www.onefpa.org/journal/Pages/APR17-Cognitive-Decline-The-Importance-of-Awareness-and-Advance-Planning.aspx

McCoy, K. (2018). 7 Key Facts About Divorce After Long Marriages. *Psychology Today.* https://www.psychologytoday.com/us/blog/complicated-love/201809/7-key-facts-about-divorce-after-long-marriages

Moore. A. (2018). *This is Why Baby Boomers are Divorcing at a Stunning Rate.* MarketWatch. https://www.marketwatch.com/story/your-failing-marriage-is-about-to-make-the-retirement-crisis-worse-2017-03-13

Planning for Diminished Capacity and Illness (2015). Consumer Financial Protection Bureau. https://files.consumerfinance.gov/f/201505_cfpb_consumer-advisory-and-investor-bulletin-planning-for-diminished-capacity-and-illness.pdf

Polyak, I. (2014). *Widows: Don't Let Grief Cloud Financial Judgement.* CNBC. https://www.cnbc.com/2014/07/10/widows-dont-let-grief-cloud-financial-judgment.html

Rehl, K.M. (2019). *Working with Widows.* The MDRT Blog. https://www.imdrt.org/blog/working-with-widows/

Rusoff, K. (2019). *The 3 Stages of Widowhood, and How Advisors can Help. Think Advisor.* https://www.thinkadvisor.com/2019/02/20/the-3-stages-of-widowhood-and-how-advisors-can-help/

Saxe, J. (2019). Planning for Diminished Capacity. *Financial Advisor.* https://www.fa-mag.com/news/planning-diminished-capacity-45536.html

Schnaubelt, C. (2018). Understanding the Financial Risks of Diminished Capacity. *Forbes.* https://www.forbes.com/sites/catherineschnaubelt/2018/06/20/understanding-the-financial-risks-of-diminished-capacity/#463397975285

Seven Steps to Protect Against Cognitive Aging (2018). *AAII Journal,* 60(9), p.5. https://www.aaii.com/journal/article/seven-steps-to-protect-against-cognitive-aging

Widowhood (2020). Cliffs Notes. https://www.cliffsnotes.com/study-guides/psychology/development-psychology/death-and-dying/widowhood

Widowhood and Money: Resiliency, Responsibility, and Empowerment (2020). Age Wave. https://agewave.com/what-we-do/landmark-research-and-consulting/research-studies/widowhood-lifestage-from-honoring-the-past-to-moving-forward/

Wild Card (2020). Merriam -Webster Dictionary. https://www.merriam-webster.com/dictionary/wild%20card

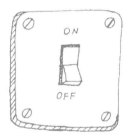

Chapter 35: Planning a Good Ending

In the final third of a person's life, it is natural—some would say even healthy—to think about and prepare for death. More specifically, think about and prepare for the way we will die and whether it will be a "good" ending to our life or a hard one. While death is certain for everyone, it is often "the elephant in the room." People avoid talking about death or issues surrounding it (e.g., funerals, obituaries, memorial services). A useful analogy for avoiding discussions surrounding death made by the British organization Dying Matters is not preparing for the birth of a child when people are expecting a baby. Birth and death still happen with or without any planning. As Benjamin Franklin famously said, "In this world, nothing can be said to be certain, except death and taxes."

So, what, exactly, is a "good death?" For many people, it means dying in peace at home, preferably surrounded by loved ones, as many celebrities reportedly do. In addition, most people want a "Niagara Falls" trajectory to their death versus a long period of increasing decline. In other words, live well for as long as possible and then "go over the edge" and die quickly. According to a 2017 Kaiser Family Foundation study, seven in 10 Americans hope to die at home versus at a hospital, hospice, or nursing home. Unfortunately, almost the reverse actually occurs. Half die in nursing homes and hospitals with 10 percent shuttled between these two facilities during their final three days of life. Furthermore, nearly half of dying Americans are subjected to uncontrolled pain.

End-of-life setting aside, another characteristic of a "good ending" is completing emotional tasks like "burying hatchets" and telling other people "thank you," "I love you," "please forgive me," and "I forgive you" before it is too late. Some people go even further and write an extended letter to their loved ones to say goodbye and/or tell others what they mean to them. Online resources like the "Friends and Family Letter template" from Stanford Medicine can help people organize their thoughts. The template includes seven prompts, including "Remember treasured moments from your life," "Apologize to those you love if you hurt them," and "Tell your friends and family how much they mean to you." The letter can be tailored for people who are healthy or dying and does not have to wait to be composed until someone is ill or on their deathbed. Legacy books (e.g., StoryWorth) and videos are other ways to leave something lasting for loved ones.

In addition to resolving disputes and saying goodbye, other ways to end life well include: being treated with dignity, pain control, spiritual and/or emotional support, access to hospice care in any location (e.g., at home or in a hospice facility), and having advance directives (e.g., living will and health care power of attorney) in place to avoid a "hospital hallway huddle" by stressed out relatives and doctors and to ensure that your personal wishes are respected. Also important are handing over control of financial and health care decisions to trusted people (versus state-appointed representatives), reviewing and updating beneficiary designations on life insurance policies and retirement accounts, sharing plans for a memorial service agenda and charitable tribute contributions, selecting and prepaying funeral and burial services, and asking proxies to promise not to prolong life needlessly.

Another way people take charge of their personal "ending" is by writing their own obituary. Homegrown obits are more likely to be published in small, rural area newspapers than urban ones but can also be placed online on a funeral home webpage and/or a website that survivors create where there is no word limit or per-word or column-inch publication fee. In addition to standard information (announcement of death, brief biography, listing of family members, and funeral information), obituary writers can add information about their passions, quirks, opinions, and accomplishments. Here is an excerpt from an obituary written by a deceased colleague:

"Expressions of sympathy may be made to MoveOn.org or other non-profit organizations that Republicans term 'Socialist' and that seek to keep banks, Wall Street, insurance companies, politicians, and other traditionally greedy and untrustworthy groups in line." He clearly had the last word and made his political viewpoints known!

Some people add advice to their obituary (e.g., "make someone smile every day") or make personal requests. For example, Sonia Elaine Todd, who died of cancer at age 38, wrote a now-famous obituary asking readers to do things, like forgive someone, quit smoking, and volunteer, in her honor. Check with newspapers(s) you plan to publish in for style guidelines and length restrictions. Some people write two obits: a standard one for newspapers and a longer, more personal obit for online distribution, sometimes as part of a tribute website with photos and videos of the deceased. Like "farewell" letters, there are online resources to help write an obituary. For example, ObitKit® provides a workbook to gather details about a person's life.

Suitable housing arrangements are also part of a good ending. Some older adults may have several homes if their need for care and supervision increases. Viewed on a continuum from no care required to skilled nursing care, options include living independently in a current home, including houses in 55+ (a.k.a., active adult) retirement communities (i.e., "aging in place"); house sharing with others; living with family members (e.g., adult children); assisted living facilities; continuing care retirement communities or CCRCs (a.k.a., life plan communities); and nursing homes. The latter three housing options require living in a group setting where institutional rules (e.g., meal times) apply. In these institutions, you might also face a lack of privacy (e.g., facility employees frequently entering a resident's living unit), necessitating proactive strategies to secure personal information and valuables.

- **Envision a Good Ending**—Decide what "a good ending" means to you and work backwards to create a list of tasks to complete to make it happen. For example, you might decide to write your obituary, prepay a burial or cremation, plan your memorial service, and reconnect with someone you severed ties with 20 years ago.

- **Take Action**—Plan as much as you can with legal documents, "to do" lists, prepaid services, conversations with advisors and surrogates, and housing choices. For example, if you are an elder orphan "ant" and have ample resources, you might elect to live in a CCRC to eliminate uncertainty about future care needs.

- **Tie Up Loose Ends**—Do what you need to do to make amends for the past and plan for an uncertain future. Examples include re-establishing relationships with others, preparing a suite of legal documents (will, durable power of attorney, living will, and health care proxy), and communicating final wishes to others.

- **Prepare a "To Do List"**—Make a list of tasks for friends or family members to perform after you pass away. Examples include contacting employers, Social Security, a pension provider, and/or financial institutions to inform them of your death and donating or distributing personal possessions.

- **Organize Financial Records**—Prepare a one-stop location (e.g., file cabinet) for documents, such as insurance policies, recent (past seven years) income tax returns, and bank, investment, and credit card statements. In this location, also leave a current net-worth statement and names and contact information for financial advisors.

- **Appoint Quality Surrogates**—Choose trustworthy people with the skills needed to manage your financial affairs and the backbone to speak up for you when you can no longer make health care decisions.

- **Change Housing as Needed**—Anticipate that you could have one or more housing changes in later life. For example, you might go from independent living to assisted living to a nursing home. Some changes may be voluntary and others not. Research housing options carefully and make a move before you are too frail to decide.

References

Butler, K. (2019). Preparing for a Good End of Life. *The Wall Street Journal.* https://www.wsj.com/articles/preparing-for-a-good-end-of-life-11549643346

Butler, K. (2019). *How to Prepare for a Good End of Life.* Fosters.com. https://www.fosters.com/news/20190304/how-to-prepare-for-good-end-of-life

Death and Taxes Quotes (2020). Brainy Quote. https://www.brainyquote.com/topics/death-and-taxes-quotes

Hiss, K. (NN). 16 Things Smart People Do for End of Life Planning. *Readers Digest.* https://www.rd.com/advice/relationships/how-prepare-for-death/16/

Housing Options for Older Adults (n.d.). National Association of Area Agencies on Aging (n4a). https://www.n4a.org/files/HousingOptions.pdf

How to Plan for a Good Death (2020). The Art of Dying Well. https://www.artofdyingwell.org/what-is-dying-well/planning-a-good-death/how-to-plan-a-good-death/

How to Write a Great Obituary (2020). Funeral Basics. https://www.funeralbasics.org/write-great-obituary/

How to Write an Obituary- A Step-By-Step Guide (2020). The Remembrance Process. https://www.remembranceprocess.com/capturing-a-life-in-words/guide-to-writing-an-obituary/

Kaiser/Economist Survey Highlights Americans' Views and Experiences with End-of-Life Care, with Comparisons to Residents of Italy, Japan, and Brazil (2017). Kaiser Foundation. https://www.kff.org/other/press-release/

kaisereconomist-survey-highlights-americans-views-and-experiences-with-end-of-life-care-with-comparisons-to-residents-of-italy-japan-and-brazil/

Passaro, J. (2018). *Why Would You Write Your Own Obituary?* https://dearpersonobits.com/blog/why-would-you-write-your-own-obituary/

Preparing for a Good Death (2018). Dying Matters. https://www.dyingmatters.org/event/preparing-good-death

Seven Keys to a Good Death (2014). Greater Good. https://greatergood.berkeley.edu/article/item/seven_keys_to_good_death

7 Ways to Prepare for Death That Will Change Your Life (2020). HuffPost. https://www.huffpost.com/entry/death-letter_n_57d1dfece4b06a74c9f3dc92

Smith, R. (2000). A Good Death: An Important Aim for Health Services and for All of Us. *BMJ*, 320(7228), 129-130. https://www.ncbi.nlm.nih.gov/pmc/articles/PMC1128725/

Stanford Medicine Letter Project (2019). Stanford Medicine. https://med.stanford.edu/letter/friendsandfamily.html

Todd, S. E. (2013). My Obituary. *Moscow-Pullman Daily News*. https://dnews.com/obituaries/sonia-elaine-todd-of-moscow/article_62ee647d-3cdb-5f84-8e9e-07983e27d156.html

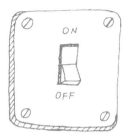

Final Thoughts

So much has happened in the eight months (September 2019 to April 2020) that I researched and wrote *Flipping a Switch*. Personally, I moved 1,100 miles from New Jersey to Florida and successfully transitioned from my role as a university professor to a financial education entrepreneur. At the same time, the country experienced multiple mass shootings (September and October 2019), media attention to the "OK Boomer" phrase (November 2019), the start of a novel coronavirus (COVID-19) in China (December 2019), and the Dow Jones Industrial Average (DJIA) index reaching a milestone 29,000 for the first time ever (January 2020).

Then things went south…very quickly. COVID-19 reached the U.S. (January 2020), killed the first American (February 2020), and was declared a pandemic by the World Health Organization (March 2020). Stock market volatility accelerated with the stock market reaching, and then exiting, bear market territory in a matter of 11 days before stock prices plunged again (March 2020). The DJIA index closed out the first quarter of 2020 at 21,917, down 23 percent for the quarter, and wide swaths of the economy are shuttered in an attempt to slow the spread of COVID-19 through social distancing. As I review this final chapter on May 30, 2020, a record 40 million Americans have filed for unemployment benefits, and the U.S. currently has more confirmed COVID-19 cases (over 1.8 million) than any country in the world and has recorded over 105,000 deaths. Even more frightening is the fact that the duration, severity, and lethality of COVID-19 are unknown at this time.

What does COVID-19 have to do with the 35 "flipped switches" you read about earlier? Actually, quite a bit. First, it was a "lens" that informed the final chapters, especially Chapter 33, *Invincible to Vulnerable.* While many baby boomers resented being called "elderly," the pandemic brought our health vulnerabilities into sharp focus. Second, I realized that some "switches" that older adults face were issues people of all ages were experiencing due to the virus. In some ways, socially distanced workers were forced into an "early retirement." Examples of "switches" that retirees and COVID-19-battered Americans had in common were creating a "paycheck," adjusting to a changed income, becoming fraud bait, avoiding too much "togetherness," keeping busy, and staying socially connected (albeit at a physical distance). Finally, I learned that my great-grandparents (parents of my grandmother with the prohibition era Irish whiskey still) died of Spanish Flu in 1918. COVID-19 is personal because I don't want a new global pandemic to kill me or another family member. Our investments will likely recover at some point, but loss of human life lasts forever. I hope that readers of *Flipping a Switch* navigated COVID-19 unscathed by death. If not, my sincere condolences to those who experienced the loss of a loved one.

Flipping a Switch concludes with 20 summary comments, insights, and recommendations in no particular order:

1. Anticipate an adjustment period. Whether you prefer to call it retirement or not, the time following a long-time career is a process, not an event. It is one of the most potentially disruptive times in a person's life and ranks #10 on the Holmes and Rahe Stress Scale of 43 stressful life events. Other events that often occur in later life are up there, too: death of a spouse (#1), divorce (#2), death of a close family member (#5), change in financial state (#16), and change in residence (#32). "A good retirement" entails more than adequate savings. Finances, physical health, and strong interpersonal relationships are the legs of a "three-legged stool."

2. Plan to spend down. Even more important than the amount of money you manage to accumulate is what you actually do with it. As this book has repeatedly advised, someone will eventually spend your money if you don't. "Ants" (or anyone, for that matter) cannot take it with them. Now is the time to arrange for memorable family experiences, consider philanthropic gifts, and explore long-term care options and older-adult housing facilities. Accept that there is a lot that you can't predict (few non-epidemiologists saw COVID-19 coming!) and adapt as necessary. The alternative is to live a life filled with anxiety, fear, and extreme caution.

3. Expect that expenses will continue to shift during two to four decades of post-work life. For example, travel expenses may decline in the "slow-go" years with less spending on cruises, airline tickets, hotels, and more. When people give up the keys to their car, money that is saved on gasoline, auto insurance, and maintenance can pay for a lot of taxi cabs or ride-sharing trips. Health care expenses often increase with age and may crowd out other spending. Income and assets can also change over time after events like gray divorce, widowhood, and inheritances. Some older adults enter retirement comfortably and die either wealthy or in poverty.

4. Never stop learning, so you can grow to be an interested and interesting person. This is hard to do when you are constrained by a tight budget with no wiggle room to try new activities or pursue new opportunities. Fun stuff costs money. Try to achieve financial independence before exiting the workforce completely. Accumulate an adequate nest egg and/or predictable streams of income, such as annuities and a defined benefit pension. Also consider some type of continued employment or self-employment for additional income and daily structure. Identify your skills, what you really care about, and what you like to do.

5. Avoid two common retirement errors: expecting you will be happy with 100 percent leisure time and assuming you can live solely on Social Security. Both of these assumptions will likely be disappointing.

Many retirees report feeling restless and bored after leisure activities, like golf, become routine. Happiness wanes unless they replace the sense of identity, intellectual stimulation, accomplishment, and daily social interaction that a job provides. Social Security was only designed to be a base of income to build upon and replaces no more than 40 percent of pre-retirement earnings and even less for higher income workers.

6. Plan for higher income taxes in the future, especially when required minimum distributions kick in. We already know that marginal tax rates will increase in 2026 if the Tax Cuts and Jobs Act is not extended. In addition, the federal deficit will be increasing significantly as a result of the $2 trillion Coronavirus Aid, Relief and Economic Security (CARES) Act designed to mitigate economic damage caused by COVID-19 social distancing. Now is a good time to fund tax-free Roth IRA accounts and municipal bonds and to make Roth IRA conversions when tax rates are low.

7. Keep a large cash stash (up to five years of income not covered by other sources such as Social Security, a pension, or an annuity) in a money market fund, high-yield savings account, or certificates of deposit to ride out periods of extreme market volatility, such as the wild swings in stock market indexes in March 2020 related to uncertainty about COVID-19. You want to be able to withdraw a regular amount of income, like a paycheck during your working years, and not worry about taking out cash for living expenses during volatile markets or a prolonged stock market downturn.

8. Work proactively to develop and maintain a post-work life social network. It is often harder to make friends when people get older because they lose the natural social "connectors" of child- and work-related activities or are inhibited by limited mobility or health-related issues. Strategies to consider are regular video-conferencing with family members (get a free Zoom account at www.zoom.com), getting a dog (pets

are great connectors), joining interest groups, attending community activities, and volunteering.

9. Transfer important activities from work life to post-work life, so retirement does not seem so disorienting. According to research studies of Continuity Theory by Robert Atchley, preserving existing life structures can enhance personal well-being. Continuity is an excellent adaptive strategy for post-work life because it does not require a host of major changes. Instead, family and volunteer roles, job-related skills, professional relationships, and/or other pursuits transition into post-retirement activities. With a strong work orientation, this is the path that I chose as a financial education entrepreneur, and I have not once felt bored or unhappy.

10. Anticipate periods of intense caregiving in later life, sometimes multiple times or for multiple generations. For example, a new neighbor in Florida experienced the widowhood of her mother and college-age children sent home due to COVID-19 within the same week! A 2018 study by the TransAmerica Center for Retirement Studies found that one in four retirees have dedicated a significant amount of time serving as a caregiver to a family member or friend who needs help taking care of themselves. At these times, planned travel and ongoing activities, volunteering, or employment often take a back seat.

11. Give serious thought to your new identity: what you are losing and who you will become. This is especially true for people with a strong work orientation who are looking for new challenges and sources of meaning and purpose. Expect to figure it out over time. This excerpt from a Marketwatch piece states it well: "Many people are simply not psychologically ready to retire, even if they're financially able. Their job is their identity. They believe that 'I work, therefore I am,' and its plaintive corollary 'Without work, what am I?'"

12. Think about your legacy. While a financial legacy (e.g., gifts and inheritances) is nice and estate planning is important, there is much more to

building a legacy than transferring money. A legacy is how you impact others: as a parent, sibling, co-worker, community member, volunteer, thought leader, and more. It is how people will remember you (e.g., kind, caring, smart, helpful, etc.) and speak about you after you pass away. Thinking about your legacy and how you want to be remembered can inform future actions to make it happen.

13. Practice mental accounting if you find it difficult to "flip the switch" from saving to spending. If you are reluctant to spend accumulated savings and see balances go down, try living only on "new" money, at least until you must take required minimum distributions (RMDs). A basic premise of this book is that it is very difficult for prodigious savers to reverse decades of thrifty habits, so don't try—at least not right away. Instead, leave savings and securities alone and try living first on Social Security, pension benefits, mutual fund distributions, stock dividends, interest, annuity payments, and post-retirement employment earnings.

14. Spend money on others if you have difficulty spending it on yourself. Findings from studies about happiness indicate that spending on others creates more happiness than self-focused spending. People often report feeling "a warm glow" when their personal resources are used to help others. In addition, spending money on experiences, such as cruises and travel, provides greater happiness than spending on possessions. Consider paying for others to join you on a vacation to combine three sources of happiness in one activity: spending money on others, a memorable experience, and spending quality time with family or friends.

15. "Test drive" heirs while you are still alive. First, make sure you have a current will that names individuals and/or organizations to be your heirs. Otherwise, state intestacy laws determine which relatives will receive your assets and how much. Charities you might otherwise have supported if you had prepared a will receive nothing. Whether you plan to leave money to people or organizations, gift them a small amount (for individuals, up to the annual gift tax exclusion; $15,000 in 2020)

and see what they do with it. If you feel they have used your money wisely, this will give you the confidence to make additional gifts. If not, you might consider some type of a trust arrangement that disburses money gradually via a trustee.

16. Create your own pension. According to the Pension Rights Center, only 22 percent of all workers (i.e., private sector and government workers combined) participate in a pension plan that provides a guaranteed monthly income for life based on income and years of service. That leaves the vast majority of workers wondering if their retirement savings will last as long as they do. This worry may be a factor in retirees' reluctance to crack open their nest egg and transition to spending more freely. A survey by Towers Watson found that retirees with pension or rental income are less anxious than those who live off of asset withdrawals. Aside from collecting Social Security and rental income, an immediate annuity can create a pension-like source of monthly guaranteed income. Shop around for a low-expense annuity provider.

17. Consider the special financial challenges that women face in later life, including a higher poverty rate than men, even if they were never poor before. Women are 80 percent more likely than men to be impoverished in retirement according to the National Institute on Retirement Security. Contributing factors include higher life expectancies and lower average earnings than men, less time in the labor force due to caregiving (women's careers average 29 years versus 39 years for men), subsidies for adult children, and decisions by women and their spouses about when to claim Social Security. Strategies to mitigate these challenges include working longer, post-retirement earnings, delaying Social Security benefits, and reducing expenses.

18. Don't wait until it is too late to exercise options that you can currently take advantage of. Whether it is writing a book, taking a trip, sharing family stories, or drafting a living will and discussing your wishes with a health care proxy, tick off "bucket list" or to-do list items sooner rather than later. Health and physical abilities rarely get better with

age, and nobody knows what the future holds for themselves or the world we live in. COVID-19 (both the high death count and the travel restrictions) showed us that. Some of the highest-ranked items of regrets for older adults are not traveling enough and not resolving family estrangements.

19. Be careful about early exits. In the wake of COVID-19 stock market volatility, I saw social media chatter about FIRE proponents who lived frugally and saved like uber "ants" to accumulate $1 million and "retire" by 40. Their plan was to follow the "4 Percent Rule" (which is questionable for young adults because the research behind it only assumed a 30-year post-retirement time frame) and withdraw 4 percent of $1 million ($40,000) to live on annually. Then that $1 million dropped in value to, maybe, $700,000. The take-away from this is that if you are going to depend on investment asset withdrawals to live on, especially for 40 or 50 years, set aside a large cash stash for living expenses to ride out market downturns and give stocks time to recover. As noted above (see #7), some advisors recommend saving up to five years' living expenses not covered by income sources, such as a pension or Social Security. For example, $20,000 x 5 or $100,000 if there is a $20,000 gap between living expenses and guaranteed income sources. Also consider post "retirement" streams of income as many FIRE devotees do.

20. Stay physically active as long as possible and fight to remain mobile, so you can move easily and freely without a walker, scooter, or pain. Lack of mobility impacts mental and emotional health, social connections, finances, housing options, and quality of life. Research indicates that, in addition to reversing muscle loss, reducing stress, maintaining bone health, and improving memory, regular physical activity reduces time spent living with a mobility-limiting disability. One study that defined "mobility disability" as being unable to walk a quarter mile, found that a physical activity program that emphasized walking cut disability time by 25 percent compared to a health education program. Health experts also recommend balance, strength training, and stretching activities.

The "How to Flip This Switch" section of the previous 35 chapters provided strategies to consider for each later life transition. Hundreds of action steps to personalize the content of *Flipping a Switch* were presented. Here, the format is different. Now, it's your turn to revisit these strategies and develop a personal action plan to flip the "switches" in your life. Simply reading this book is not enough to guarantee happiness and financial security in later life. You will need to work at it.

Start slowly with a few action steps and add more as you complete some activities and make progress. The goal here is not to overwhelm you but to empower you. Use the following three tables to record your plans for financial transitions, social transitions, and lifestyle transitions.

Financial Action Steps

Social Action Steps

Lifestyle Action Steps

Writing *Flipping a Switch* taught me so much about transitions that I am currently experiencing (and will experience) in later life. It provided me a reason to delve into hundreds of blog posts and research studies about issues of importance to people leaving the workforce at any age, but particularly fellow baby boomers. I hope that my hours of searching for, reading, and synthesizing data about post-career transitions is as useful to you as it was to me.

I close with this quote by Karen Salmansohn: "Anxiety happens when you think you have to figure out everything all at once. Breathe. You're strong. You got this. Take it day by day."

References

A Precarious Existence: How Today's Retirees are Financially Faring in Retirement (2018). Transamerica Center for Retirement Studies. https://www.transamericacenter.org/docs/default-source/retirees-survey/tcrs2018_sr_retirees_survey_financially_faring.pdf

Atchley, R.C. (1989). A Continuity Theory of Normal Aging. *The Gerontologist*, 29(2), 183-190. https://academic.oup.com/gerontologist/article-abstract/29/2/183/581908

Benz, C. (2020). *Retirees and Pre-Retirees: You've Got This!* Morningstar. https://www.morningstar.com/articles/974302/retirees-and-pre-retirees-youve-got-this

Burton, J. (2019). *You're Probably Not Ready to Retire-Psychologically* (2019). MarketWatch. https://www.marketwatch.com/story/why-youre-probably-not-psychologically-ready-to-retire-2019-05-21

Chevreau, J. (2020). *Is Early Retirement a Realistic Goal for Most People.* MoneySense. https://www.moneysense.ca/columns/retired-money/how-to-retire-early/

Clements, J. (2020). *Opening the Spigot.* Humble Dollar. https://humbledollar.com/2020/01/opening-spigot/

Clements, J. (2020). *5 Ways to Help You Spend Your Retirement Savings-Wisely.* MarketWatch. https://news.yahoo.com/m/05275c41-8c5f-3038-9c84-1270afddda2c/5-ways-to-help-you-spend-your.html

Coronavirus Disease 2019 (COVID-19): Cases in the U.S. (2020). Centers for Disease Control. https://www.cdc.gov/coronavirus/2019-ncov/cases-updates/cases-in-us.html

COVID-19 Coronavirus Pandemic (2020) Worldometer. https://www.
worldometers.info/coronavirus/#countries

Hannon, K. (2019). *A Dire Situation for Women's Retirement, and What's Being Done About It.* MarketWatch. https://www.marketwatch.com/story/a-dire-situation-for-womens-retirement-and-whats-being-done-about-it-2019-02-21

Helping Clients Through the Honeymoon Phase of Retirement (2020). Hartford Funds. https://www.hartfordfunds.com/investor-insight/mit/8000-days-of-retirement/honeymoon-phase.html

Henning, G., Lindwall, M. & Johansson, B. (2016). Continuity in Well-Being in the Transition to Retirement. *Journal of Gerontopsychology and Geriatric Psychiatry*, 29(4), 225-237 https://psycnet.apa.org/record/2016-58463-006

Hobson, K. (2016). *Walking Fends Off Loss of Mobility, and It's Not Too Late to Start.* NPR. https://www.npr.org/sections/health-shots/2016/09/26/495477531/walking-fends-off-disability-and-its-not-too-late-to-start

How to Increase Mobility in Older Adults (2018). Salmon Health. https://www.salmonhealth.com/blog/how-to-increase-mobility-in-older-adults/

How Many American Workers Participate in Workplace Retirement Plans? (2019). Pension Rights Center. https://www.pensionrights.org/publications/statistic/how-many-american-workers-participate-workplace-retirement-plans

Hughes, K.A. (2020). Coronavirus Has Boomers Asking: Who Are You Calling Elderly? *The Wall Street Journal.* https://www.wsj.com/articles/coronavirus-has-boomers-asking-who-are-you-calling-elderly-11584457650

Mamula, C. (2019). *Nearly 2 Years into Early retirement, Here's All That I've Gotten Wrong.* Market Watch. https://www.marketwatch.com/story/nearly-2-years-into-early-retirement-heres-all-that-ive-gotten-wrong-2019-08-19

Miller, K. (2020). How Spending Money on Others Promotes Happiness. *Positive Psychology.* https://positivepsychology.com/spending-money-promotes-happiness/

O'Neill, B. (2020). *Six COVID-19 "Flipped Switches."* https://moneytalk1.blogspot.com/2020/03/six-covid-19-flipped-switches.html

Otani, A., Isaac, A., & Chiu, J. (2020). Stocks End Worst Quarter in 12 Years. *The Wall Street Journal.* https://www.wsj.com/articles/global-stock-markets-dow-update-11585617395

Pawlowski, A. (2017). *How to Live Life Without Major Regrets: 8 Lessons from Older Americans.* NBC Today. https://www.today.com/health/biggest-regrets-older-people-share-what-they-d-do-differently-t118918

Pfau, W. (2018). How Much of Your Savings Can You Spend Each Year in Retirement? The Answer, Updated for 2018. *Forbes.* https://www.forbes.com/sites/wadepfau/2018/01/10/william-bengens-safemax-updated-to-2018/#40bf2e596be4

Quinn, R. (2019). *Update: The 10 Commandments of Retirement.* Morningstar. https://www.marketwatch.com/story/the-10-commandments-of-retirement-2018-08-21

Rosato, D. (2015). Why You Should Spend More Money in Retirement. *Money.* https://money.com/spend-money-retirement/

The Holmes and Rahe Stress Scale (2020). MindTools. https://www.mindtools.com/pages/article/newTCS_82.htm

U.S. Now Leads the World in Confirmed Cases (2020). *The New York Times*. https://www.nytimes.com/2020/03/26/world/coronavirus-news.html

Women 80% More Likely to be Impoverished in Retirement (2016). National Institute on Retirement Security. https://www.nirsonline.org/2016/03/women-80-more-likely-to-be-impoverished-in-retirement/

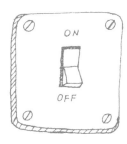

Acknowledgments

Here's hoping that my book, Flipping a Switch
Will provide you with new insights and make your life rich

Not just financially, but your lifestyle too
It is your future to decide what is important to you

Knowing "switches" ahead can help you make plans
To shape your life to be the best that it can

Thank you, dear readers, for taking time out of your day
To read my book and hear what I say

Many people shared ideas to inform this book.
Below is a list; please give it a look.

I would like to extend my gratitude to the following individuals and organizations:

- To my deceased parents, Mary W. O'Neill and Francis X. O'Neill who role-modeled the value of engaging in hard work and becoming an "ant."

- To my husband, Gene M. Bronson, who has supported my dreams, goals, and accomplishments for 43 years.

- To Rutgers University, a generous employer that provided me with opportunities to do creative and impactful work and achieve financial independence.

- To the following individuals who provided helpful input and insights into the content of *Flipping a Switch*: Rosella Bannister, Patricia Q. Brennan, Cindy Cannelongo, Fran Coletti, Jonathan Clements, the late Jeff Daly, Joseph DiFiglia, Don Blandin, Maryanne Evanko, Carole Glade, Sally Gibson, Tau Guo, Lacey Langford, Lori Lucas, Beatrice May, Sharon Nikaido, Jamie Novak, Michael O'Neill, Joseph Ponessa, Jane Schuchardt, Pamela Weiss, Leila Wissert, and the late Paul Westbrook.

- To the following organizations that provided me with opportunities to discuss the content of *Flipping a Switch* in articles, webinars, and podcasts: American Association of Family and Consumer Sciences (AAFCS), Association for Financial Counseling and Planning Education (AFCPE), eXtension Financial Security for All Community of Practice (FSA CoP), New Jersey Foundation for Aging (NJFA) and the Military Money Show. I also appreciate the insights and support of members of the FinCon Authors Helping Authors Facebook group.

- To Doug Brown and Jack Bussell of Atlantic Publishing for greenlighting my book concept without even a sample chapter to review, Katie Cline for her expert project management support and copy-editing, and Jessie Ranew for her assistance with marketing *Flipping a Switch*.

- To Don Blandin for writing an outstanding foreword and for his ongoing support throughout this project.

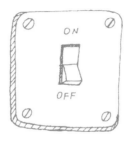

About the Author

Barbara O'Neill, Ph.D., CFP®, AFC®, CRPC®

Dr. Barbara O'Neill, CFP®, AFC® is the owner/CEO of Money Talk: Financial Planning Seminars and Publications where she writes, speaks, and reviews content about personal finance. A Distinguished Professor Emeritus at Rutgers University, after 41 years of service as a Rutgers Cooperative Extension educator and personal finance specialist, she has written over 160 articles for academic publications and received over 35 national awards and over $1.2 million in grants to support her financial education programs and research. Dr. O'Neill is a past President of the Association for Financial Counseling and Planning Education (AFCPE), a recipient of the AFCPE Distinguished Fellow Award, and a Next Gen Personal Finance fellow. She tweets personal finance information using the handle @money-talk1 and writes weekly posts for her Money Talk blog.

Milton Keynes UK
Ingram Content Group UK Ltd.
UKHW021303251123
433259UK00022B/863